GO ▷ snow board

Neil McNab

DK

London, New York, Munich, Melbourne, Delhi

Editors **Ed Wilson, Sophie Bevan, Bob Bridle**
Project Editor **Richard Gilbert**
Project Art Editor **Mark Cavanagh**
Design by **On Fire**
DTP Designer **Vânia Cunha**
Production Controller **Elizabeth Warman**
Managing Editor **Stephanie Farrow**
Managing Art Editor **Lee Griffiths**
Photography **Gerard Brown**

DVD produced for Dorling Kindersley by
Chrome Productions www.chromeproductions.com
Director **Gez Medinger**
Camera **Neil Gordon**
Production Manager **Portia Mishcon**
Production Assistant **Gavin Rowe**
Voiceover **Trevor White**
Voiceover Recording **Mark Maclaine**
Music **Chad Hobson,** produced by **FMPTV**

First American Edition, 2006

Published in the United States by
DK Publishing, 375 Hudson Street,
New York, NY 10014

06 07 08 09 10   10 9 8 7 6 5 4 3 2 1

A Cataloging-in-Publication record for this book is
available from the Library of Congress.

ISBN-13: 978-0-7566-2357-9
ISBN-10: 0-7566-2357-X

DK books are available at special discounts for bulk
purchases for sales promotions, premiums, fund-
raising, or educational use. For details, contact:
DK Publishing Special Markets, 375 Hudson Street,
New York, NY 10014 or SpecialSales@dk.com

Color reproduction by Icon Reproduction, UK
Printed and bound in China by Hung Hing

Discover more at

www.dk.com

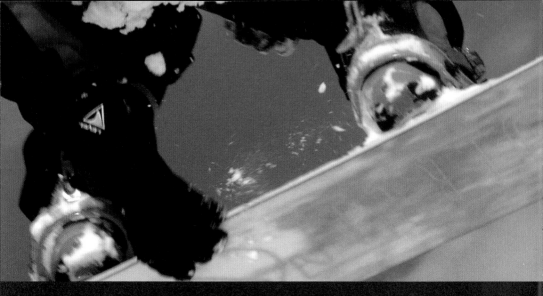

contents

How to use this book and DVD 10
Why snowboard? 12

GO FOR IT **14**
Coming up... 16

The goal
A moment in freeriding 18

The theory
Understanding the theory 22

Mountain safety
Staying safe on the mountain 26
Piste safety 28

GO GET YOUR GEAR **30**
Coming up... 32

Essentials and extras
Essential gear 34
Added extras 36

Board and bindings
Snowboard technology 38
Selecting your board 40
Bindings 42

Boots and clothing
Boots 44
Clothing 46

GO FIND YOUR FOUNDATIONS **48**
Coming up... 50

The stance
Understanding the stance 52
Setting your stance to the board 54
Strapping into your board 56

Getting on
Preparing for movement 58
Getting up and falling down 60

Starting to move
Climbing and skating 62
Straight running 64

GO LEARN THE BASICS **66**
Coming up... 68

Moving on your board
Side-slipping—heel edge 70
Side-slipping—toe edge 72
Diagonal side-slipping—heel edge 74
Diagonal side-slipping—toe edge 76
Falling leaf—heel edge 78
Falling leaf—toe edge 80
Garland—heel edge 82
Garland—toe edge 84

Making turns
First turn—heel 86
First turn—toe 88
Using the whole mountain
Linking and progressing 90
Riding lifts 92

GO BEYOND THE BASICS **94**
Coming up... 96

The McNab Pressure Control System
Introducing the control points 98
Working the control points 100

Pressure control
Refining pressure transfer 102
Using opposing pressure 104
Building pressure control 106
Wait, don't rotate 108

Edge control
Precise steering 110
Edging and balance 112
Riding fakie 114

Sharper steering
The funnel 116
The corridor 118

GO FURTHER **120**
Coming up... 122

Terrain and conditions
Variable terrain 124
Speed awareness 126
Speed control—the theory 128
Speed control—the practice 130
Variable conditions 132
Riding powder 134
Powder techniques 136

Freestyle
Introducing freestyle 138
Ollies 140
Kickers 142
Grabs 144

Freeriding
Introducing freeriding 146
Freeriding—the tips 148
Freeriding—the techniques 150

More stuff
Snowboarding on the Net 152
Board talk 154
Index 156
And finally... 160

how to use this book and DVD

This fully integrated book and accompanying DVD are designed to inspire you to get out onto the slopes. Watch all the essential techniques on the DVD in crystal-clear, real-time footage, with key elements broken down in state-of-the-art digital graphics, and then read all about them, and more, in the book.

Using the book
Venturing onto the slopes for the first time can be a daunting prospect, so this book explains all you need to know to snowboard with safety and confidence. Cross-references to the DVD are included on pages that are backed up by footage.

Switch on the DVD
When you see this logo in the book, check out the action in the relevant chapter of the DVD.

Using the DVD

Supporting the book with movie sequences and computer graphics, the DVD is the perfect way to see key techniques demonstrated in precise detail. Navigate to each subject using the main menu, and view sequences as often as you like to see how it's done!

Flick to the book
When you see this logo on the DVD, flick to the relevant page of the book to read all about it.

why snowboard?

Snowboarding combines the natural flowing ride of the
surfer, the raw, dynamic creativity of the skateboarder,
and the skillful, high-performance mountaincraft of
the skier to offer the mountains' ultimate experience.
Nothing beats the feeling of powering down the side
of a mountain, cutting graceful arcs through deep,
fresh snow, using the natural camber of the terrain
to carve, drop, and spin off as you charge down the
mountain under the effortless pull of gravity.

In this book you will see how to take your first
steps into this exciting world of high mountains,
challenging descents, and awesome airtime.
You will learn that snowboard technique is a simple
science, combining the natural movements of the
body, the design technology of the board, and the forces
of nature. This book and accompanying DVD will help you
learn and understand the skills needed to safely reach
a high level of snowboarding. From the all-important
foundations, to the demanding arts of freeriding and
freestyle, Go Snowboard teaches you the natural way to ride.

Neil McNab

go for it!

coming up...

The goal: 18—21

Snowboarding combines the flowing ride of the surfer, the dynamic creativity of the skateboarder, and the mountaincraft of the skier to create the mountains' ultimate ride. Learn how to carve the pistes, drop the drops, and charge the steeps.

The theory: 22—25

Snowboard technique is a simple science, combining the natural movements of the body, the design technology of the board, and the flowing forces of nature. Understanding the theory will teach you the natural way to ride, how to turn your board by design rather than by force, and help you progress swiftly toward the highest levels of the sport.

Mountain safety: 26—29

Snowboarding is practiced in a very unforgiving and often demanding high-mountain environment that requires a certain degree of care and safety. A few simple tips will help make your time in the mountains a safer and more pleasurable experience.

a moment in freeriding

The fresh snow glitters in the bright sunlight, coating the mountain with a smooth blanket of white. The air is still, the sky a perfectly clear blue. Tall, jagged pillars of granite thrust toward the skyline. Beneath my feet, the mountain terrain rolls endlessly down toward the valley below. I am alone, surrounded by nature, waiting in the stillness of the high-altitude air.

I look down over the terrain below, considering the possibilities before me. I breathe in the stillness of the mountain, and then, when the moment feels right, I turn my board toward the valley, releasing myself to the pull of gravity.

My speed builds rapidly as I carve down the steep, wide slope. I make a deep turn to the left, causing a thick veil of powder snow to arc into the air from beneath my board, a white curtain that momentarily hides the valley from view as I cut back across the slope, changing direction. I ride up a steep bank on the left, watching the lip, waiting for the

continued >

a moment in freeriding (continued)

feeling of weightlessness to arrive, and then I slash the crest of the wave of snow, filling the sky with crystals. Launching off a drop, I pull my board up underneath me, grabbing the edge with my rear hand, floating, weightless—time seems to stand still until gravity takes hold again and I begin to drop. I hold on until the last second before releasing the grab, touching down, pushing the pressure through my back foot to keep the nose of the board up as snow explodes into the air. I straight line out into the sunshine and ride into the valley far below.

This is snowboarding at its best, the ultimate descent. You feel charged with energy, you're traveling fast but your mind is clear, and your movements are precise and calm. You feel in perfect harmony with your board, and the ever-changing terrain of the mountain as you ride, leaving your signature on the snow.

Snowboarders are always searching for this perfect descent. Everyday you practice you'll get a little closer, but everyday your expectations grow, and your goals are pushed a little farther out of reach. This is the journey, the search for perfection, and the closer you get, the farther away it seems. You may never make the perfect descent, but you will have a lot of fun along the way.

understanding the theory

continued >

The techniques discussed in this book are based on a combination of simple biomechanics (how the body moves and balances), simple physics (the most efficient way for momentum to change), and snowboard technology (manipulating the board by design rather than force). If we can understand these three elements, and explore how they function, we can fit them together to create the perfect snowboard technique.

Biomechanics
Everyone needs to follow the same basic rules when it comes to snowboarding. You must bend and flex in the same way for balance, and make the same pressure-control movements with your feet to manipulate the board into and out of turns.

Center of gravity
Your center of gravity is situated just below your navel. When your body is relaxed, it will adjust naturally to keep you balanced over your feet.

Controlling the board
The movements needed to control and turn your board are very subtle, and come from your feet. Use small, precise foot movements rather than big, forceful body movements.

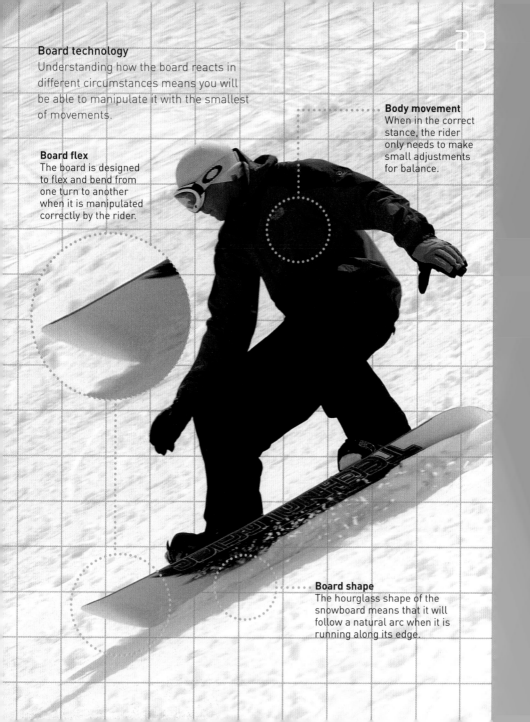

Board technology
Understanding how the board reacts in different circumstances means you will be able to manipulate it with the smallest of movements.

Body movement
When in the correct stance, the rider only needs to make small adjustments for balance.

Board flex
The board is designed to flex and bend from one turn to another when it is manipulated correctly by the rider.

Board shape
The hourglass shape of the snowboard means that it will follow a natural arc when it is running along its edge.

understanding the theory (continued)

The physics of the turn
The most efficient way to change momentum in order to turn is by performing an arc or curve. With the correct technique, you'll be able to make effortless smooth, rounded arcs as you flow down the mountain.

Balancing forces
By leaning inside the turn, the body is naturally balanced and counteracts the forces applied to it by the turn acting against it.

Turn shape
The smoother and more rounded the curve, the easier and more efficient the turn.

Putting it all together
By understanding and combining the physics, biomechanics, and technology of snowboarding, you'll be able to ride the mountain efficiently and effortlessly.

Center of gravity
Your center of gravity is situated here. Relax in a natural stance and your body will balance itself.

Body movement
If correctly aligned over your feet, your knees will flex naturally to help you balance.

Foot movement
Your feet are the interface between you and the board. Focus all your board-control actions through your feet.

Path of travel
Try to follow a smooth arc, or curve, in order to make your turns effective and efficient.

Flexing the board
If you manipulate (flex and steer) the board correctly, it will turn by design rather than force.

staying safe on the mountain

Snowboarding is often performed in harsh conditions, and you should never underestimate the dangers of the high-mountain environment. Although you can expect to find more forgiving surroundings within the boundaries of the ski area (shelter and first aid, for example), always be prepared for the dangers posed by this changeable environment.

Watching the weather

There is a 2°F drop in temperature for every 300 ft (100 m) of vertical height gained. Even if it is relatively warm in the valley, expect much cooler conditions up on the mountain, and dress accordingly. The wind plays a huge part in the cooling process, and the wind-chill effect can have serious consequences. Chair lifts often leave you exposed to the elements, and the enforced inactivity brought about by sitting in a chair lift can make it very difficult to keep warm.

Essential safety tips

Here are three simple, but vitally important, steps to take for a safe day's riding.

- Drink fluids regularly throughout the day. The air on the mountainside is dry and harsh. As you will be engaged in a demanding sporting activity, expect to become dehydrated quickly. Re-hydrating drinks with electrolytes are highly recommended.

- Wear a strong, protective sunscreen on exposed areas of skin at all times. On the mountain, the snow acts as a giant reflector, meaning there is 80 per cent more UV radiation than in the valley. Even on cloudy days, UV rays will filter through the clouds.

- Take it slowly for a few days, especially if you come to the mountains from a relatively low-lying area. The higher the altitude, the less oxygen there is in the air. Your body will need to work harder just to maintain its normal functions.

piste safety

The piste operates in much the same way as a wide road with one-way traffic. When joining, setting off, climbing, or stopping on a piste, always make safety a priority. Try to anticipate the actions of your fellow piste users, and familiarize yourself with the International Ski Federation (FIS) rules of conduct for skiing and boarding. Be aware that pistes are color-coded using an international scale, ranging from green for easier slopes, to black for the most difficult (see page 155).

Looking around

Always look uphill before setting off or joining a piste, and stop in a place where you can easily be seen—clear of blind spots. If possible, pull up at the side of the piste. If there's a group of you, keep close together so as not to obstruct the path of others. Heed the rules and advice of the ski patrol.

Accidents

In the event of an accident, everyone is duty-bound to help, if help is needed. Make sure that the area is made safe, and clearly signal the obstruction to other piste users. Talk reassuringly to the injured party, make them as comfortable as possible, and insulate them from the cold conditions. Gather information about what has happened, where the incident is located, and the type of injuries involved, then call for the ski patrol. If other people are there to help, send two people together to call for the ski patrol, who can be reached from every lift station.

Rules of the piste

- Behave with respect; never endanger others.
- Stay in control. Adapt your speed to suit your ability, the conditions, and how busy it is.
- When approaching from behind, choose a route that doesn't endanger those ahead.
- You may pass on the left or the right, but allow space for other users of the piste.
- When entering a piste, or setting off after stopping, check up and down the slope first.
- Avoid stopping in narrow places on-piste, or where visibility is low.
- When climbing and descending on foot, use the side of the piste.
- Respect all signs and markings on the piste.
- At accidents, you are duty-bound to assist, and exchange names and addresses.

coming up...

Essentials and extras: 34–37

Some of the equipment you will need is specific to the high-mountain environment, while some is specially designed with snowboarding in mind. Here you will learn what to look for when choosing your equipment.

Board and bindings: 38–43

What you ride is just as important as how you ride it! If your gear isn't up to the job, then you won't be either. Choosing the right board and bindings will make your time on the slopes a lot easier, and a lot more enjoyable.

Boots and clothing: 44–47

Snowboard clothing is specifically designed to suit the demands of the snowboarder and the high-mountain environment. Snowboard boots are designed to help you transfer your riding skills to the board while keeping your feet warm and comfortable. There's a range of choices, so here's what you should be looking for.

essential gear

Snowboarding is practiced in a very unforgiving and often demanding high-mountain environment and requires equipment that is specific to the sport. Snowboard gear is designed to be both fashionable and functional, and is constructed using specialist techniques and materials.

Much of the gear featured here will be covered in greater detail in later chapters, but these are all of the essential items that you will need. As a rule, when buying equipment, you should always consider your ability, your body measurements, your particular snowboarding interests, and how much you can realistically afford to spend.

Hat
Up to a third of your body heat is lost through your head. A good hat that covers your neck is vital.

Bindings
Your bindings are the direct interface between your boots and your board. A good pair of bindings will enhance your ability to ride and progress.

Safety leash
A leash is used to attach your board to your front foot or leg, to stop it from sliding away.

Board
Your board has no brakes, so always place it upside down, and in a safe place, when you're not using it out on the mountain.

Boots
Your boots should be warm, comfortable, supportive, and waterproof.

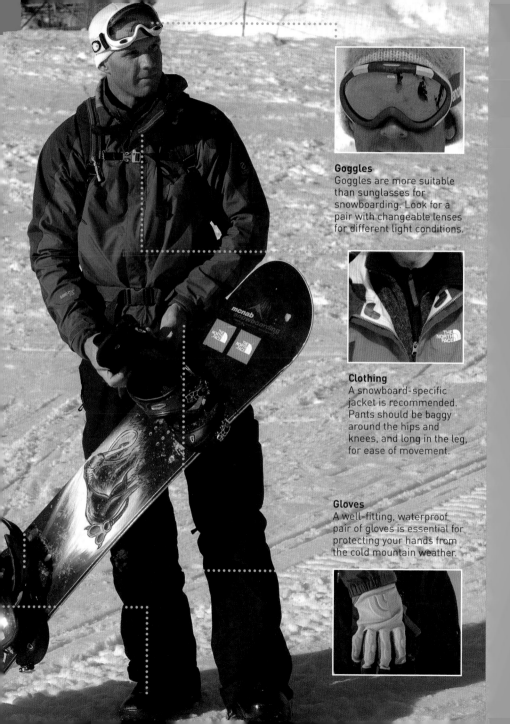

Goggles
Goggles are more suitable than sunglasses for snowboarding. Look for a pair with changeable lenses for different light conditions.

Clothing
A snowboard-specific jacket is recommended. Pants should be baggy around the hips and knees, and long in the leg, for ease of movement.

Gloves
A well-fitting, waterproof pair of gloves is essential for protecting your hands from the cold mountain weather.

added extras

In addition to the snowboarding essentials that will get you started on the slopes, it is worth considering some extras that will make your time on the mountain safer and more enjoyable. Body protectors and a basic maintenance kit are useful in all riding environments, while special avalanche safety gear is essential for the adventurous snowboarder riding off-piste.

As you learn to snowboard, you will inevitably take the odd tumble, so good protective gear is a wise investment. A pair of wrist guards, for example, is particularly important to protect you when falling forward. Here are some more items you should consider.

Impact protection

Many riders wear protective body armor for everyday riding. Snowboarding can be a high-impact sport, but there is protective equipment available to help reduce the risk of injury. Back protectors and impact shorts are highly recommended, and wrist guards are an important piece of safety equipment. If possible, it's worth trying them on in the shop to make sure they will fit under your gloves! Impact protection vests are also available. They have built-in shoulder, elbow, and back protection, and are great for a day in the terrain park.

Other useful equipment

If you plan to ride off-piste, even within the patrolled ski area, always carry the correct avalanche safety equipment, and know how to use it. A maintenance kit is also a useful addition.

- A shovel, probe, and transceiver (an electronic position locator) are all essential avalanche rescue gear.

- Avalanche safety reflective detection patches integrated into some snowboard clothing are a minimum safety requirement for off-piste riding.

- Bindings can come loose, so a bindings screwdriver is particularly useful.

snowboard technology

A snowboard is designed to glide down the mountain and turn when manipulated correctly by the rider. The techniques covered in this book will help you learn to turn your snowboard by design rather than by force. Most boards have very similar design features, which are highlighted here. Understanding the theory behind how the board is designed to work will help your progress when you are strapped in and riding on the mountain.

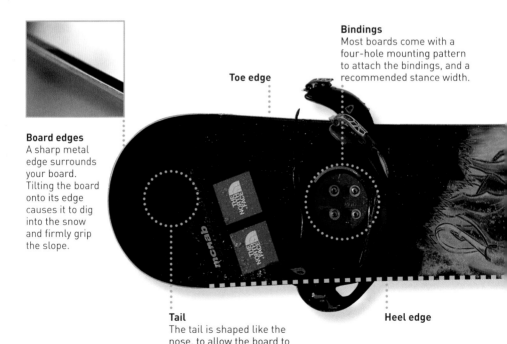

Bindings
Most boards come with a four-hole mounting pattern to attach the bindings, and a recommended stance width.

Toe edge

Board edges
A sharp metal edge surrounds your board. Tilting the board onto its edge causes it to dig into the snow and firmly grip the slope.

Tail
The tail is shaped like the nose, to allow the board to be ridden backward.

Heel edge

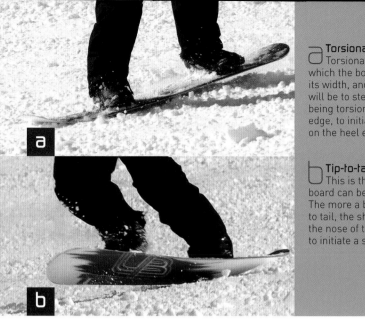

Torsional flex
Torsional flex is the extent to which the board can be flexed across its width, and determines how easy it will be to steer. Here the board is being torsionally flexed from the toe edge, to initiate a steering movement on the heel edge.

Tip-to-tail flex
This is the extent to which a board can be flexed along its length. The more a board is flexed from tip to tail, the sharper it will turn. Here the nose of the board is being flexed to initiate a sharp, small-radius turn.

Width
Boards come in various widths to suit the size of your feet. Your toes and heels should extend to the edge of the board, but no farther.

Control points
The control points, found at the four corners of the board, are used for steering, by transferring pressure between them (see pages 98–99).

Sidecut
The curved edge shape is called the sidecut and enables the board to turn as it runs along its edge. The deeper the sidecut, the more sharply the board will turn.

Nose
Most snowboards have a raised nose called a shovel. This helps the board stay on top of the snow.

selecting your board

When deciding what kind of snowboard to use, you need to choose the type that suits your skill level, build, and interests.

If you are a beginner, look for a board with softer flex properties as this makes it easier to ride. Your build also plays a big part in your choice—a heavy rider will need a stiffer board than a lighter rider, while a taller rider will generally need a longer board than a smaller rider. Female-specific boards are also available. The final factor is the type of riding you want to do— "freestyle" (in the terrain park) or "freeride" (all-mountain).

Board width
Your boots should come to the edge of the board but no farther, so you can apply pressure to the edge in a turn. Boards come in "mid-wide" and "wide" for riders with larger-than-average feet.

Freestyle board
At home in the terrain park and ideal for beginners, freestyle boards tend to be short with soft flex properties. This makes them easier to maneuver, but less stable at higher speeds.

Shorter board
Short length makes turn initiation easier.

Soft flex
Soft boards are more maneuverable on snow and in the air.

Bidirectional
Symmetrical in design, twin-tip freestyle boards feel the same when ridden forward or backward.

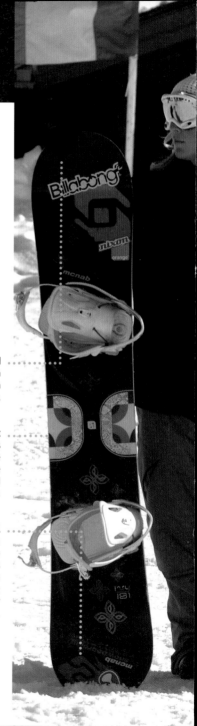

Freeride board

Generally longer in length with stiffer flex properties, freeride boards are designed to go anywhere, whether you want to carve up the piste, ride the powder, or catch some air. Some freeride boards are wider, and have more volume in the front than the rear, to aid with flotation in deep powder.

Longer board

A longer edge makes the board more stable at high speed.

Stiff flex

Stiffer boards are harder to maneuver, but more stable at higher speeds.

Directional

Directional boards are softer in the nose than the tail, making turn initiation easier, and giving more power to the end of the turn.

how bindings work

Your bindings form the interface between you and the board. They transfer the precise movements you make with your feet directly to where they are needed to control the board.

Bindings need to fit well and be comfortable, adjustable, supportive to the biomechanics of your stance, and performance-oriented. A useful feature to look for is a raised "gas pedal", which is used for applying toe-edge pressure. Any unnecessary movement between your feet and the bindings will quickly translate into a loss of precision in your riding.

There are two popular types of bindings available—the step-in binding, and the two-strap binding (shown here). While both have their advantages and disadvantages, for performance purposes the two-strap binding is recommended.

Bindings in detail

• The most important part of the binding is the high back, or spoiler. It should be high, comfortable, and supportive, with adjustable forward lean.

• Most bindings use a four-hole disk to adjust stance width and center each boot between the toe and heel edge. Binding angles are also set using this disk.

• Screws on bindings can become loose, so check them regularly. If they are loose, tighten them with a screwdriver.

• Make sure the toe and heel straps on your binding are comfortable, fully adjustable, and easy to use.

Padded high back
(also known as spoiler)

High back controls
heel-edge pressure

Forward-lean
adjuster

Anatomically shaped and
padded heel strap

Ratchet strap closure

Anatomically shaped
base plate

Comfortable
toe strap

High-back
rotation
adjustment

Raised "gas pedal"

boots

Boots should be warm, waterproof, comfortable, supportive, and hard-wearing. There are many different boots available on the market, and, as with the bindings and board, they are designed to suit different standards of riders and different styles of riding.

When buying boots, it is a good idea to go to a well-established snowboard shop, where staff will be able to guide you to the right boot for your needs. Boots are designed specifically for male or female riders to help you get the perfect fit. They also come with different degrees of stiffness and a range of lacing systems. If you use step-in bindings, you will need boots specifically designed to work with them.

Finding a good fit
Take your time when choosing your boots—a good fit is vital for comfort and performance. Look for a boot to suit your personal riding standard and experience. A softer boot is more forgiving of clumsy technique but less precise, while a stiffer boot offers greater precision, but is much less forgiving. Your boot should hold your heel and foot snugly. Most snowboard boots come with removable inner boots, some of which can be molded for a custom fit, which is good for frequent riders. A molded inner sole is essential for both comfort and precision. The lacing system of your boots should allow you to custom-fit the foot and cuff independently for a precise fit.

Tongue
The tongues of your boots need to be adequately stiff to offer support to your stance, while allowing you to flex freely for balance.

Heel
The heel of the boot gets a lot of abuse from the binding, so hard-wearing protection is important.

Grip
The boot should have good grip for walking, be flat to fit your binding, and have heel cushioning to soften impact.

**go find your
foundations**

Useful features

You don't need countless features on your clothing, but the following are recommended:

- Underarm, chest, and thigh vents are important features to look for in a jacket and snowboard pants—they allow your body to breathe.

- A powder skirt that attaches to your pants will keep out deep snow.

- Ankle gaiters keep the snow out of your boots; velcro cuffs will seal your wrists; and an adjustable hood with a high neck keeps the snow out on top.

- About one-third of your body heat is lost through your head, so look for a warm, tight-knit hat.

- Snowboard pants with a baggy fit allow you greater freedom of movement.

clothing

Snowboard clothing combines developments in high-performance mountain wear with the latest high-street trends—it is both function-oriented and fashion-conscious. Good snowboard gear is designed to withstand the rigors of the sport and keep you warm and comfortable on the mountain, no matter what the conditions.

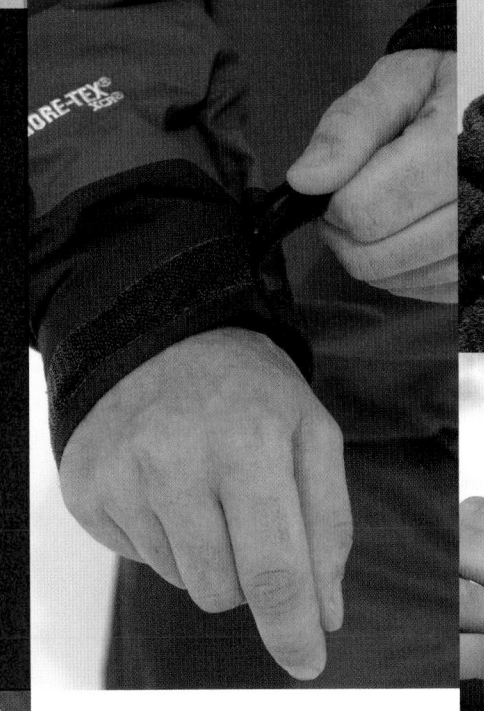

Layers

A light and well-designed layering system is highly recommended. Choose layers that can be easily adjusted to suit the changeable conditions on the mountainside.

Base layer
A thermal wicking layer next to the skin keeps your body warm and dry.

Mid-layer
Soft-shell mid layers are great for sunny days, while a thicker fleece will keep you warm when it's cold.

Outer layer
This layer keeps out the elements. Look for a snowsports- or mountain-specific lightweight shell jacket that is both waterproof and breathable.

Inner lining
Most boots have a removable inner boot that has an independent lacing system. This is essential for a high-performance fit.

Upper lacing system
Locking cleats allow for a custom fit around the lower leg for support and comfort.

Lower lacing system
Running eyelets allow the tension to be evenly distributed over the foot.

coming up...

The stance: 52–57

The basic stance is the single most important element in snowboarding. Based on simple biomechanics, it's the cornerstone on which your technical foundations will be built. Getting your basic stance right is the key to your future progression.

Getting on: 58–61

The second most important factor in snowboarding is setting up your equipment correctly. Ill-fitting equipment will make your time on the snow more demanding, both physically and mentally, and your progress will suffer.

Starting to move: 62–65

Before you take on the steep and the deep, you need to get the basics under your belt. The more skillfully you can operate at this most basic level, the stronger and easier your progression will become. Take your time and don't rush!

understanding the stance

The stance is the single most important element in snowboarding. A good stance, based on simple biomechanics, is the key to progress. It is important that you understand the intricacies of the stance from the start, since any irregularities that develop during these early stages will hinder you later on.

Finding your stance width

You need to be able to direct pressure through your feet, toward the nose and tail of the board. Place your feet at different widths apart, until you find a position that feels strong and comfortable. Practice moving pressure from one foot to the other, feeling for how you create and transfer the pressure, using both feet in opposition to each other. If your stance is too narrow, your hips will move, and you'll be manipulating the board with body weight, rather than foot pressure. If your stance is too wide, your natural body movements will feel restricted.

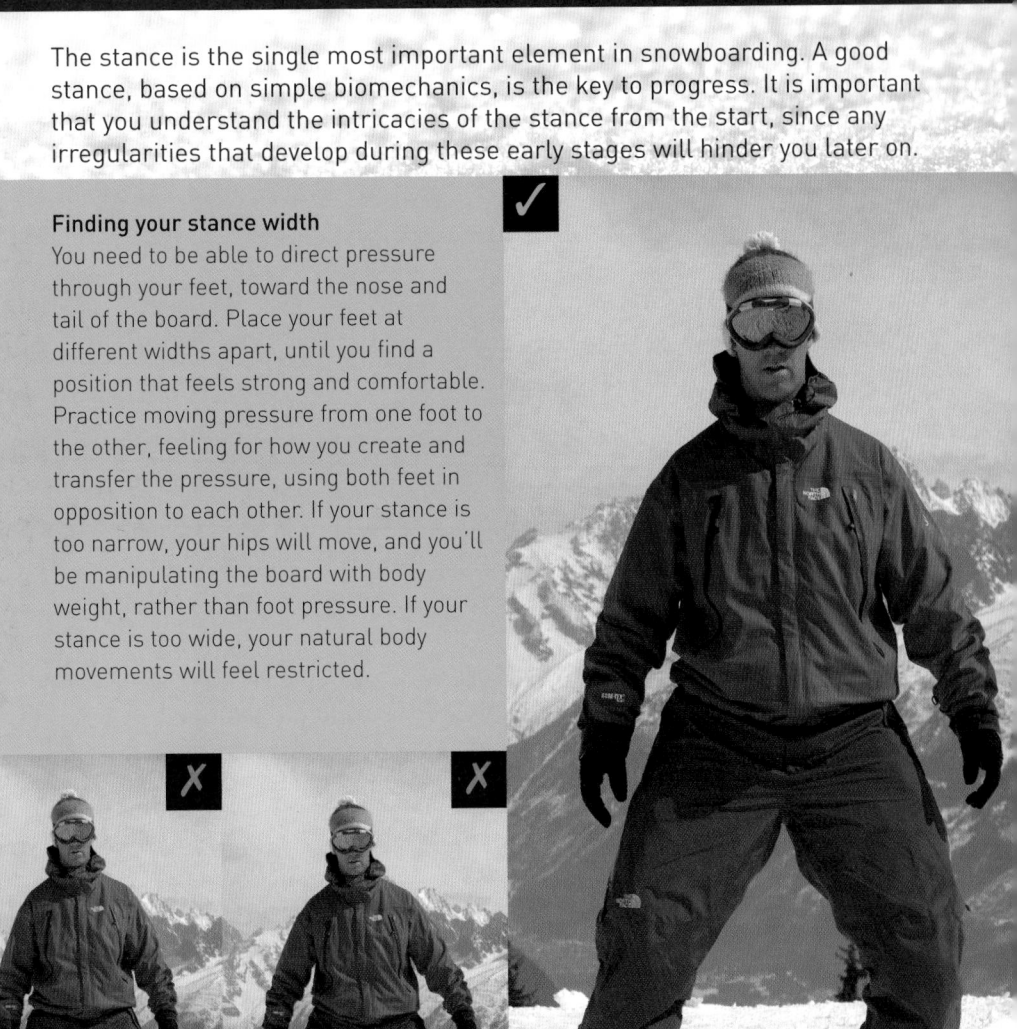

WATCH IT
see DVD chapter 1

a Normal stance angle

Once you've set your stance width, you need to set your stance angle. To do this, line up your feet with your thighs so that when you bend your knee and ankle joints they are not under undue pressure. For most people, the angle between both feet is 20–30°.

b Narrow stance angle

Many boarders slightly reduce the angle difference between their feet, as this creates more pressure in the outside edges of the feet. You do, however, need some angle difference to work the nose and tail of the board, flex naturally, and see where you're going.

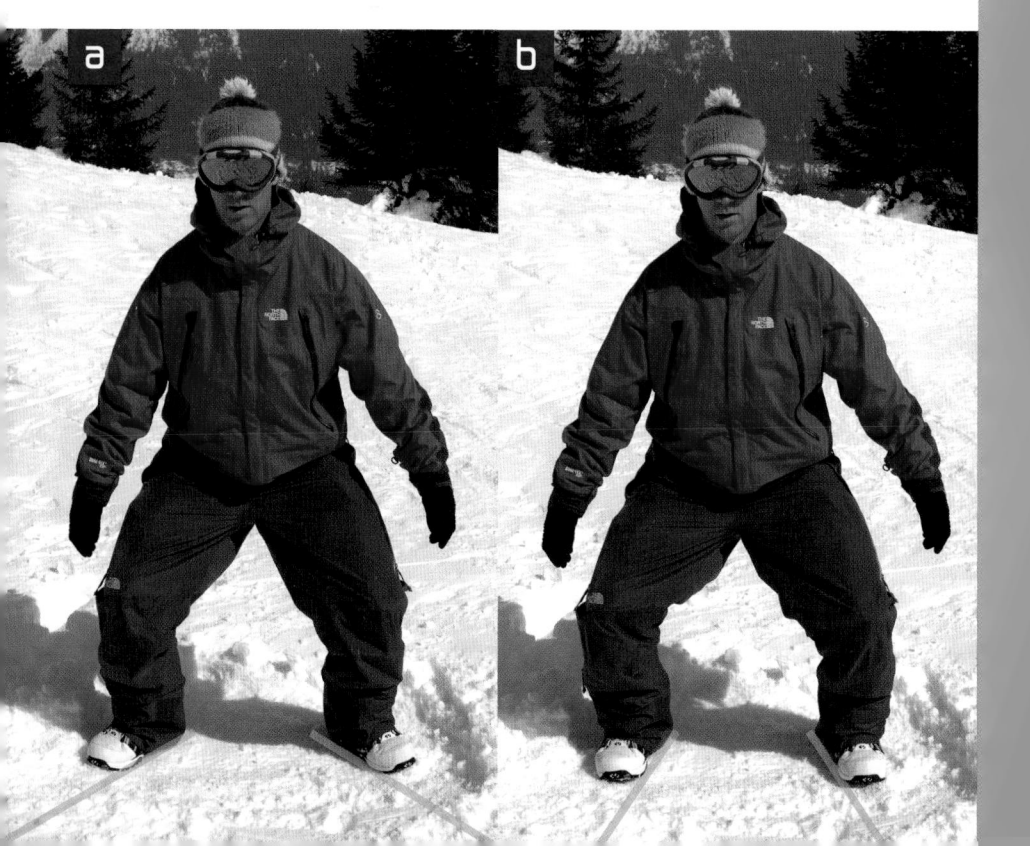

setting your stance to the board

Once you have a good feel for the stance away from your board, it's time to apply the same principles while standing on it. You need to find out if you're regular or goofy, set your stance width on your board, and work out your binding angles—an essential part of how you ride and control the board.

Your front foot angle, facing slightly forward, determines field of view (how much you can see without turning your hip), and controls pressure to the front of the board. To control pressure in the rear of the board, your back foot should face slightly backward. Keep the angle difference you found in your perfect stance, and apply it on the board.

Am I regular or goofy?
To find out which position is best for you—regular (left foot forward) or goofy (right foot forward)—think how you would stand on a skateboard, or slide on ice. Alternatively, ask someone to push you from behind. The foot you instinctively step forward onto is your forward foot.

Field of vision
Your field of vision is determined by the binding angle of your front foot. The narrower the angle, the less you'll be able to see without turning your hip.

Binding angles

The manufacturer of your board will provide guidelines for a recommended stance width. Use this to stay central, making equal lateral adjustments to both bindings for a wide, powerful stance.

- Use the holes in your binding disks to micro-adjust your stance width. Most have angle guides in 3° increments.

- These holes also center your boot, so that your toes and heels reach either edge evenly.

- Adjust the forward lean on your high backs, to give you heel-edge support.

- Most riders use around −6° on their back foot (measured perpendicular to the length of the board). The front foot is around +20°. This angle difference provides effective pressure control, and a good field of view.

strapping into your board

You can strap into your board while standing or sitting. Initially, it may be easier to sit down, since you don't have to balance and your board can't move around. Strap your front foot in first, fastening the heel strap and then the toe strap. Repeat this procedure with your back foot. There are different types of bindings, but the most common method of attachment is shown here.

3 When your front foot is securely in place, clip the clasp of your leash to a point on your boot, such as one of the lace loops.

4 Now, place the back foot into the rear binding. Remember to make sure your pants leg is not caught in the binding.

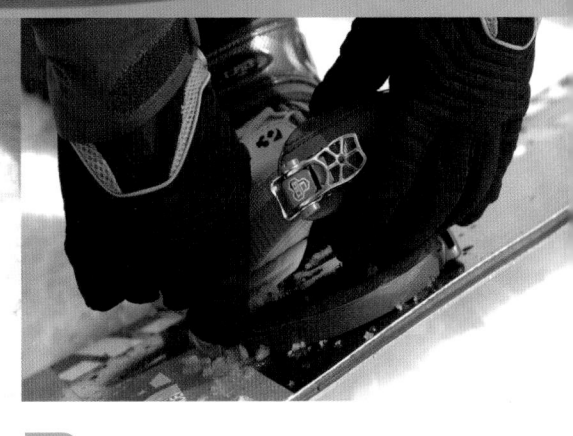

1 Strapping into the board
Check that your pants leg is free of the binding. Push the heel of your front foot firmly into the back of the base plate, leaving no gap between your boot and the binding, and fasten the heel strap.

2
Once the heel strap is secure, fasten the toe strap firmly, fixing your front foot securely in the binding.

5
Fasten your heel strap firmly, then your toe strap. Be sure there is no movement between your foot and the binding.

6
When both feet are strapped into the bindings, check that they are snug. Make sure there is no movement between your foot, your boot, your binding, and your board.

preparing for movement

Once you're on your board, you'll need to familiarize yourself with your stance, and explore some of the basic movements you'll need when you start to ride. Learn to relax over your feet, and feel how your body balances. Try to become aware of how precise movements in your feet control your whole body from the feet up, rather than from your head down. Understanding these principles will put you in a stronger position once you start to ride.

Flexion and extension

Flexion and extension are the body movements that keep you balanced as you ride. Relax, and become familiar with the feel of your body balancing over the board. Start at your feet and work upward, noticing how your limbs and joints feel when strapped into the board. Flex up and down by bending your knees, keeping your head upright, your knees apart and your center of gravity balanced over the middle of the board.

Pressure

The way you distribute pressure with your feet controls the board as you ride. Gently roll your feet outward, feeling pressure build naturally in the outside edges of both feet. Direct the pressure evenly toward the nose and tail of the board. Now slowly move the pressure from nose to tail. Don't move your hips—work only with your feet, rolling pressure from the nose to the tail repeatedly.

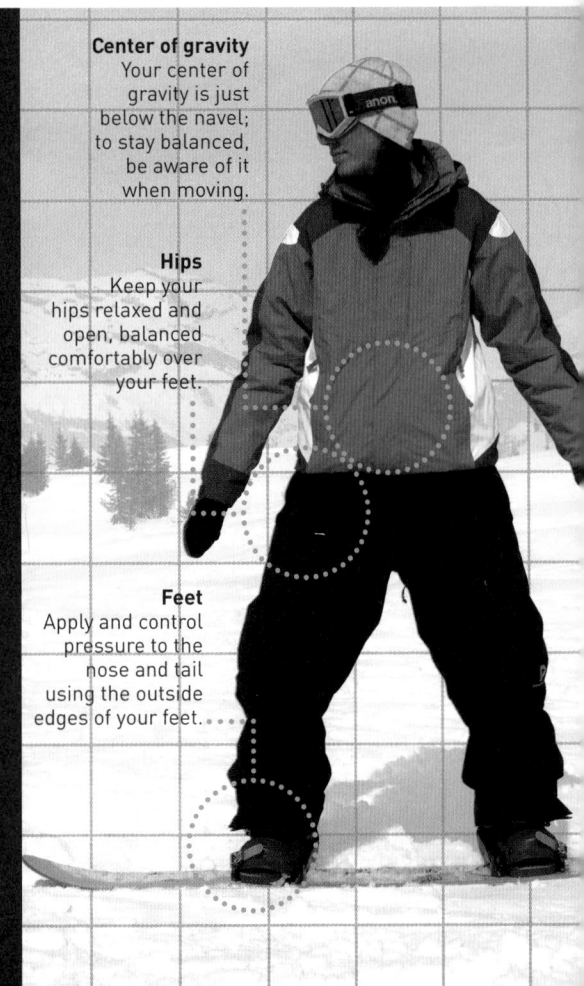

Center of gravity
Your center of gravity is just below the navel; to stay balanced, be aware of it when moving.

Hips
Keep your hips relaxed and open, balanced comfortably over your feet.

Feet
Apply and control pressure to the nose and tail using the outside edges of your feet.

How not to do it

If your shoulders and hips are turned toward the front of the board, it will disrupt your body mechanics and create tension within your stance. It will pull the pressure control away from your feet, and draw the board toward the heel edge, turning even the simplest task into a battle between you and the board. Keep your body relaxed and aligned correctly over your feet, turning only your head in your direction of travel.

X

Eyes
A horizontal eyeline helps you maintain balance.

Head
Only your head should turn toward your path of travel, not your whole body.

Arms
Your arms should be by your side, relaxed but ready for use.

Knees
Your knees should be softly flexed and over your feet. Allow them to flex naturally for balance.

getting up and falling down

Once you've attached both feet into your bindings, getting up can be quite awkward, and requires some practice. When you're upright, it's quite likely that, at some point, you will fall down. In the beginning, you should get someone to help you stand up and balance.

Most people find it easier to get up on their toe edge. If you've just put your board on sitting down, you're probably on your heel edge. This means you will have to turn over. With practice, you'll be able to get up from both edges easily.

Falling

When you're learning to snowboard, it's quite common to fall over—normally not through choice. If you feel yourself falling, crouch down, keep your arms out of the way, and roll onto your back. As soon as you make contact with the ground, lift your board off the snow and keep your body soft. Always think, "Go low and soft"!

Tuck your arms in

Bend your knees

Getting up onto the heel edge

1 With the board across the slope, dig your heel edge in. Push up using one arm.

2 Lever yourself up, using one hand to push, with the other hand in front of you to balance, until you can stand up.

3 Stand up straight, balancing gently over your heel edge. The more you dig the board into the slope, the easier this is.

Getting up onto the toe edge

1 With your board pointing across the slope, dig your toe edge in. Put your hands in front of you and push up.

2 With your center of gravity moving over the board, push your knees apart, and control the toe edge with your feet. Begin to stand up straight.

3 Balance over your toe edge, and stand up. Keep even pressure across the board through both feet.

climbing and skating

Your first exercises on your board should be performed on flat or very gentle terrain, and will involve learning how the board works, slides, and glides. These initial exercises will be performed with your back foot free, and with only your front foot strapped into its binding.

As you learn to snowboard, you need to become familiar with your gear. You will use the techniques covered here a lot in the future, to get around on flat and uphill sections, and these early exercises provide the technical foundations on which everything else is built. Getting a feeling now for how the board glides, and how its edges can be pressured to control movement, will make things easier when both feet are strapped onto the board.

1
Climbing
Begin facing uphill with your board across the slope. Your back foot, free of its binding, should be placed in front of the toe edge.

2
Stand on your board's toe edge with your front foot, ensuring it grips the snow. Take a small step up the slope with your free foot.

3 Move your body weight over your free foot and lift your board up the slope to join it.

4 Return the board to the starting position, keeping it perpendicular to the slope. Repeat the sequence.

WATCH IT see DVD chapter 1

Skating

1 Practice skating on flat terrain. Start with your back foot free and the board flat to the snow.

2 Balance over your front foot. Bring your back foot forward on the toe edge to push yourself forward.

3 Let the board glide and repeat the pushing action. Take small steps, pushing harder as your confidence grows.

straight running

Once you've practiced climbing and skating, the next step is straight running. You should try this on very gentle ground, with your back foot free at first. Then, as you gain confidence, attempt the exercise with both feet attached to the board.

For straight running, we introduce the idea of the "fall line." This is the line running straight down the slope, as determined by gravity. If you were to drop a ball on a slope, the fall line is the path the ball would take as it rolled down the hill.

1 **Straight running**
Find a slope with a slight incline and a natural stopping area—and someone to offer assistance! Start with your board pointing across the fall line.

2 With help, shift your position so that the board is now aligned with the fall line. Make sure you keep your feet, and the base of the board, flat to the snow. Hold a relaxed stance, with your legs flexed.

WATCH IT
see DVD chapter 2

3 Turn your head in the direction of travel, feeling for the correct alignment of your joints.

4 Apply slight pressure through the outside edges of your feet—to control the front of the board and move into a slide.

5 Before you come to a natural stop, try to get a feel for the opposing pressure in your back foot.

Moving into straight running
As you start skating, simply step your back foot onto the board, in between your bindings. Balance over both feet as you glide. When you feel more confident, try this on a very slight incline, and run straight down the slope with your board flat.

Free foot
Place your free foot just in front of your back binding. Use it for balance, and to move pressure forward for board control.

Front foot
Balance over both feet, but hold more pressure on your front foot for board control. Your free, back foot should work in opposition.

go learn the basics

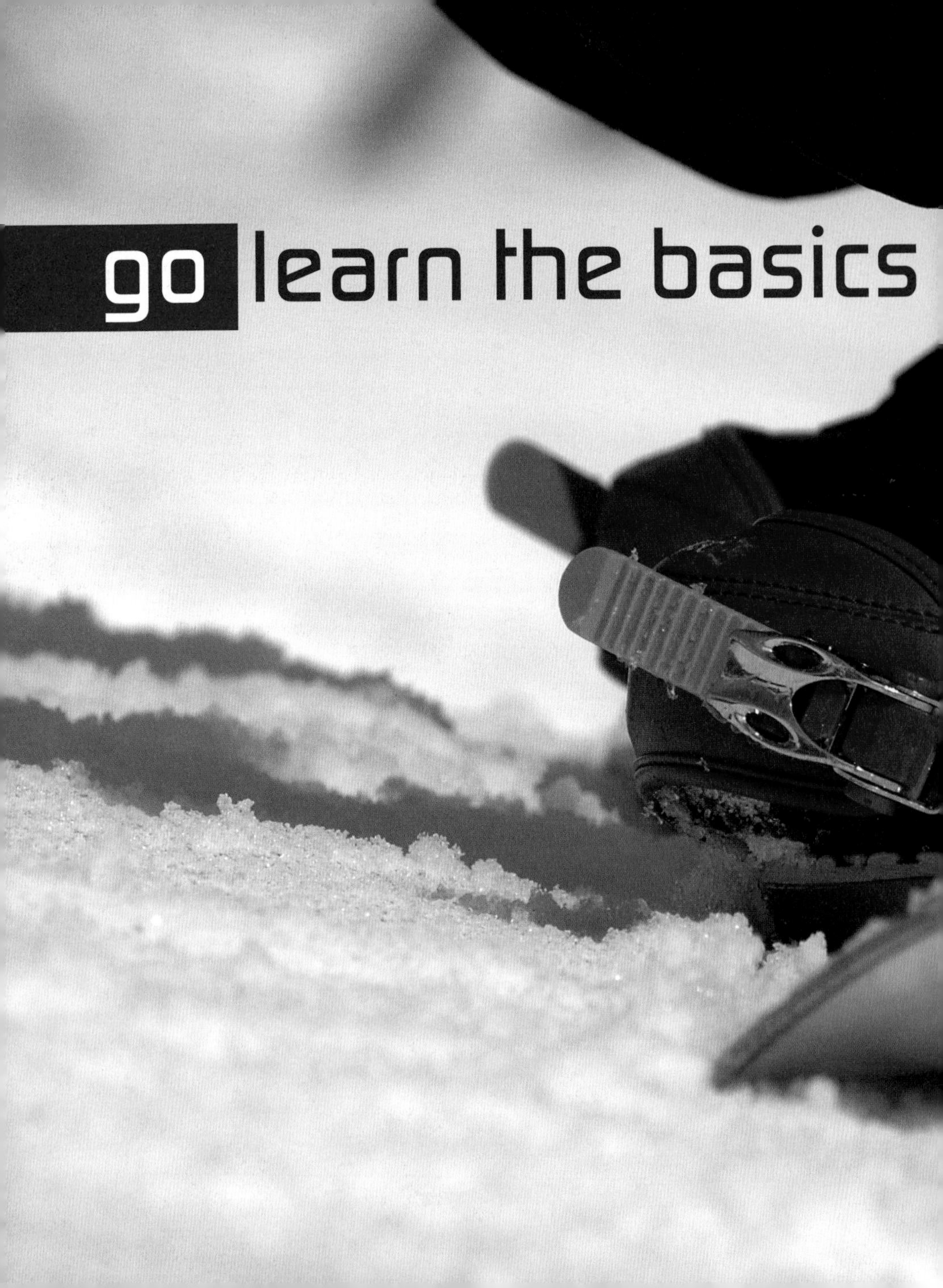

coming up...

Using the whole mountain: 90-93

When you link your first turns together, you open the door to the world of snowboarding. Everything you do from this point on is built on the foundations you have learned. Relax, and ride from your feet up, not your head down.

Making turns: 86-89

The basic turn is the end product of work on your technical foundations. If you have understood the basic progression techniques, your first turns should feel effortless, and you should be turning your board by design, rather than force.

Moving on your board: 70-85

Your technical foundations will determine how quickly you progress. Here, we introduce you to the basic technical elements of snowboarding— edge control, pressure control, and steering. Take your time, and let your knowledge grow step by step.

side-slipping—heel edge

Side-slipping is the first step toward making a basic turn. The technique introduces edge control, or edging, which describes the amount of edge tilt applied to the board. This can be along the length of the board, in line with the direction of travel (carving), or across the slope, in opposition to it (skidding).

Side-slipping uses a combination of both pressure and edging, and mastery of this technique will greatly improve your control of the board. It should be performed on shallow, open, and smooth terrain, slightly steeper than that used for straight running.

Even pressure
As you slide, apply pressure through the outside edges of your feet—by pushing your knees out—to create pressure along the working edge (in this case the heel edge).

Footwork—heel-edge side-slip

This technique employs opposing pressure control movements in both feet as you slide down the slope.

Pressure is spread toward the outside edge and across each foot evenly.

1 Heel-edge side-slip

Start from a relaxed position on your heel edge, with your board across the slope. Flex your legs for balance, applying pressure through your heels.

2

Slowly bring the pressure in the heels forward to reduce the edge tilt, and release the board's grip on the slope. As you begin to slide, extend your body for balance (see page 72). Try to keep the pressure even through both feet, and go with the slide.

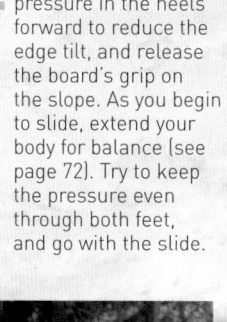

3

Gently increase the edge tilt to regain your start position, flexing for balance (see page 72). Remember to focus pressure evenly along the edge of the board, using the outsides of your feet.

WATCH IT
see DVD chapter 2

side-slipping—toe edge

Side-slipping teaches you how to move your body to maintain your balance over the edge of the board. It also teaches you the effects of pressure along the edge, and how to control edge grip by using precise movements of your feet.

Mastering the skill

The three control elements of snowboarding (edging, pressure, and steering) are applied using particular body movements. For edging, these are flexion and extension. Flexion means adopting a crouchlike position when coming to a stop. Extension is straightening up your body when moving off.

Flexion

As your body flexes to keep its center of gravity over the working edge (in this case, the toe edge), the edge tilt increases.

Extension

As your body extends, and the center of gravity moves off the edge, your feet flatten, and tilt decreases.

Footwork—toe-edge side-slip
Like the heel-edge side-slip, the toe-edge side-slip also requires opposing pressure control movements from your feet as you move through the exercise.

Pressure is spread toward the outside edge and across each foot evenly.

1 Toe-edge side-slip
Start on your toe edge, pointing across the slope. Use edge tilt to grip the slope, flex, and look up.

2 Check over your shoulder to be sure your path is clear. Gradually lessen the edge tilt to release the grip on the slope, allowing yourself to slide. Extend, or straighten, your body to maintain your balance over the edge.

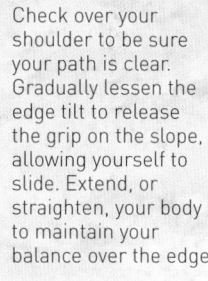

3 Increase the edge tilt to bring the slide to a stop. Use even pressure on the tip and tail of the board, flexing for balance.

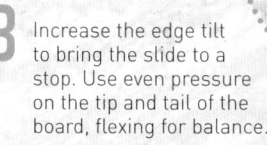

diagonal side-slipping—heel edge

Diagonal side-slipping adds the element of pressure control to the side-slip, introducing increased pressure toward either the nose or tail of the board while side-slipping. This is an essential step in your progression toward making a basic turn, and promotes diagonal direction control, as well as preparing the nose or tail of the board for further action.

Diagonal side-slipping should be performed on gentle, open, smooth terrain, as with the side-slip. Try to use the same terrain throughout so you can concentrate on the task.

Mastering the skill
Try to make all movements through your feet, keeping your body relaxed and correctly aligned. Keep your adjustments to edge control and pressure control subtle and smooth. Move just enough pressure to achieve the task—moving too much will upset the biomechanics of your stance.

Front foot
Increase the pressure to the front of the board by focusing the pressure through the outside edge of your front foot.

Back foot
The pressure bias in the front of the board is created and controlled from the opposing force in the back foot.

Heel-edge diagonal side-slip

Start in a stationary position over your heel edge. Put even pressure on the board with both feet, then slowly extend, reducing edge tilt.

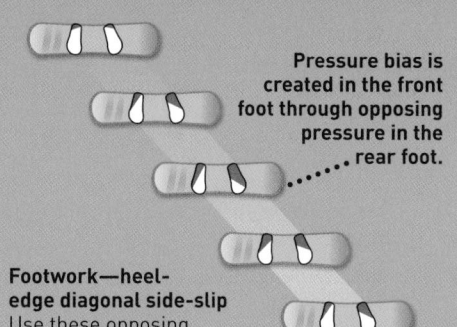

Pressure bias is created in the front foot through opposing pressure in the rear foot.

Footwork—heel-edge diagonal side-slip
Use these opposing control movements in your feet as you move through the exercise.

2 Once you are sliding, increase pressure toward the nose of the board to control direction, while releasing the edge tilt evenly with both feet to control the slide.

3 Slowly bring the pressure back to an even balance, while increasing edge tilt. Return to the starting position.

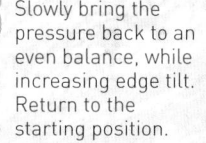

WATCH IT
see DVD chapter 2

diagonal side-slipping—toe edge

As with the diagonal side-slip on the heel edge, the toe-edge diagonal side-slip involves applying more pressure toward the front of the board to create a slight change in direction.

The diagonal side-slip introduces an essential element of the basic turn progression, and is a key technique for higher levels of riding.

It is important to create and channel all the control through your feet. Although there is more pressure focused on one foot than the other, release the edge evenly with both feet to control the slide. Keep your body relaxed and neutral.

Turning your head
Make sure you turn only your head in the direction of travel. Rotating the upper body will reduce your ability to control the board.

Toe-edge diagonal side-slip

From a stationary position across the hill, slowly release the edge pressure to begin a side-slip. Extend accordingly for balance.

Pressure bias is created in the front foot through opposing pressure in the rear foot.

Footwork—toe-edge diagonal side-slip

Apply pressure across your feet as shown, using opposing control movements to perform the exercise.

2 Using your back foot in opposition, slowly increase pressure toward the nose of the board on your toe edge. This should give a slight diagonal direction to your side-slip.

3 Slowly return even pressure to both feet, and increase the edge tilt to stop. Flex accordingly for balance.

falling leaf—heel edge

The falling leaf exercise takes its name from the pattern with which you glide down the hill. It introduces steering to the basic progression.

Steering works alongside the elements of pressure control and edge control to complete the ingredients needed for the basic turn. In this exercise, you will practice the turn-initiation process needed for the basic turn. This will provide a solid base from which to build your skills, and move into a more advanced phase of riding. As you practice the falling leaf, slowly increase the amount of steering you use and focus on making your movements fluid and precise. Your speed is controlled by how much you steer, so start off gently.

Smooth terrain
As a beginner, it's best to practice on a wide, gentle slope with plenty of room to maneuver.

Heel-edge falling leaf

From a side-slip on the heel edge, slowly add pressure with your front foot to move into a diagonal side-slip.

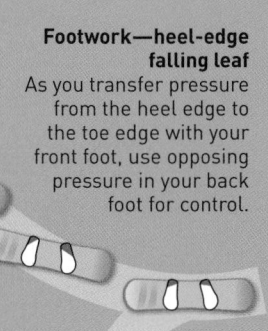

Footwork—heel-edge falling leaf

As you transfer pressure from the heel edge to the toe edge with your front foot, use opposing pressure in your back foot for control.

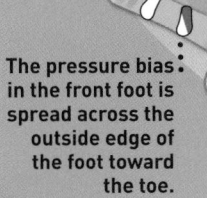

The pressure bias in the front foot is spread across the outside edge of the foot toward the toe.

2 Use a pedaling action with your front foot to transfer pressure across the front of the board toward the toe edge, bending your knees in the direction of travel.

5 Move into the heel-edge side-slip again to stop. Repeat this pattern down the slope, alternating feet.

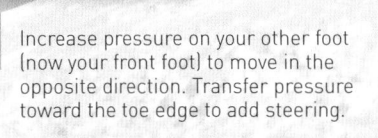

3 Let the snowboard run a little. Apply pressure to the heel of your front foot to stop sliding. Return to the start position.

4 Increase pressure on your other foot (now your front foot) to move in the opposite direction. Transfer pressure toward the toe edge to add steering.

falling leaf—toe edge

For the toe-edge falling leaf, use a pedaling movement with your front foot to steer the board from toe to heel, as you did in the heel-edge exercise. Focus this pressure toward the outside edge of your foot to take it across the front of the board.

Try to avoid upper body movement, building all your techniques from the feet up. Feel how your back foot works in opposition as you begin to torsionally flex the board to steer. Move only pressure, not weight.

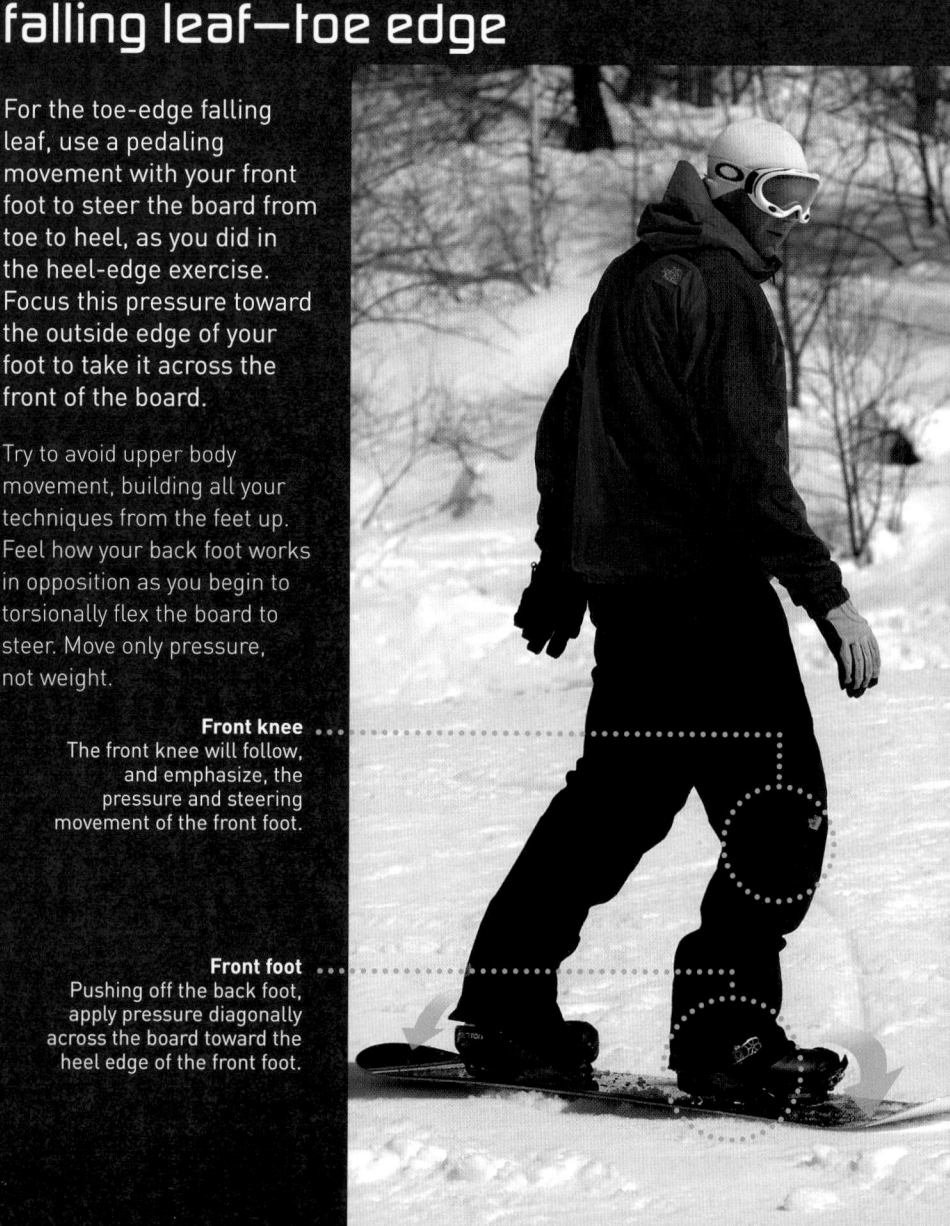

Front knee
The front knee will follow, and emphasize, the pressure and steering movement of the front foot.

Front foot
Pushing off the back foot, apply pressure diagonally across the board toward the heel edge of the front foot.

1 Toe-edge falling leaf
From a controlled side-slip, increase pressure in your front foot, as for the diagonal side-slip. Keep your speed down and get ready to steer.

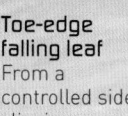
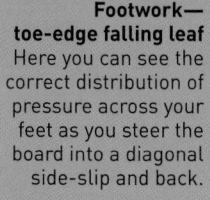

Footwork— toe-edge falling leaf
Here you can see the correct distribution of pressure across your feet as you steer the board into a diagonal side-slip and back.

The pressure bias in the front foot is spread across the outside edge of the foot toward the heel.

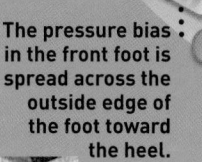

2 Slowly move pressure across the front of the board toward the heel edge. Use the board's torsional flex to steer.

5 Moving with precision, slowly bring the pressure back to your toe edge, returning to the side-slip and start position.

3 Steer down the hill, letting the board run a little before moving back into a side-slip to stop.

4 Use a pedaling motion in your new front foot to steer back across the slope.

WATCH IT
see DVD chapter 2

garland—heel edge

With the garland, you will enter a practice phase of the basic turn progression, as all of the technical ingredients are now in place. The garland is simply the falling leaf exercise repeated over and over again in a forward only direction. In addition, the board is turned further each time until it is pointing directly down the fall line of the slope. As the garland makes use of all the snowboarding techniques you've learned so far, try to get a feeling for the individual elements, and how they work together, while you practice.

1 **Heel-edge garland**
From a stationary position across the slope, reduce edge tilt to move into a side-slip, progressing to a diagonal side-slip.

2 Steer toward the fall line by pedaling with your front foot on the toe edge. Leave some pressure in your back foot for control.

3 Keep pedaling with your front foot to flatten the board toward the fall line. Extend your body for balance.

WATCH IT
see DVD chapter 2

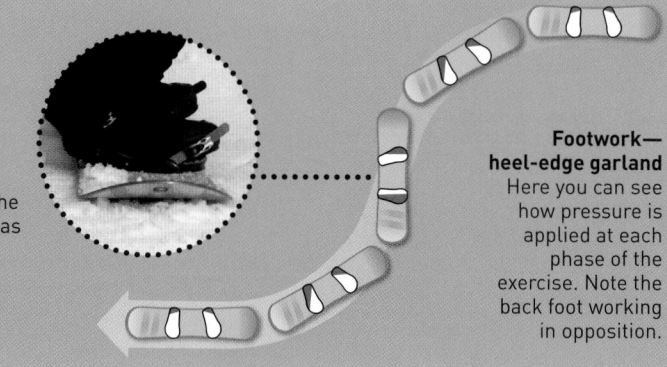

Flattening the board
Steer toward the fall line until you feel the front of the board flatten to the slope, as shown. Be aware of the opposing pressure in the back foot as you stand tall over your front foot.

Footwork— heel-edge garland
Here you can see how pressure is applied at each phase of the exercise. Note the back foot working in opposition.

4 Once you feel the board flatten into the fall line, begin to steer back toward the heel edge, arcing across the slope. Use opposing pressure in your back foot to support your front-foot steering.

5 Return to the side-slip and starting position, controlling the heel edge with even opposing pressure in both feet before repeating the exercise.

garland—toe edge

Try to recognize, understand, and work through each step in the progression as you perform the garland, building everything from the feet up. With the toe-edge garland, try to eliminate any unnecessary upper-body rotation, steering with your feet, and turning only your head in the direction of travel.

Concentrate on the opposing pressure movements in your back foot, remembering that you can't have pressure or steering in the front of the board without it. Be precise with your feet, as this is where all the control originates.

1 **Toe-edge garland**
From a stationary position, release the edge tilt to begin a side-slip. Increase pressure to the front of the board.

2 Transfer the pressure across the front of the board, pedaling your front foot from heel to toe as you steer toward the fall line.

3 Feel the front of the board flatten out, and extend your body for balance, standing tall over your front foot.

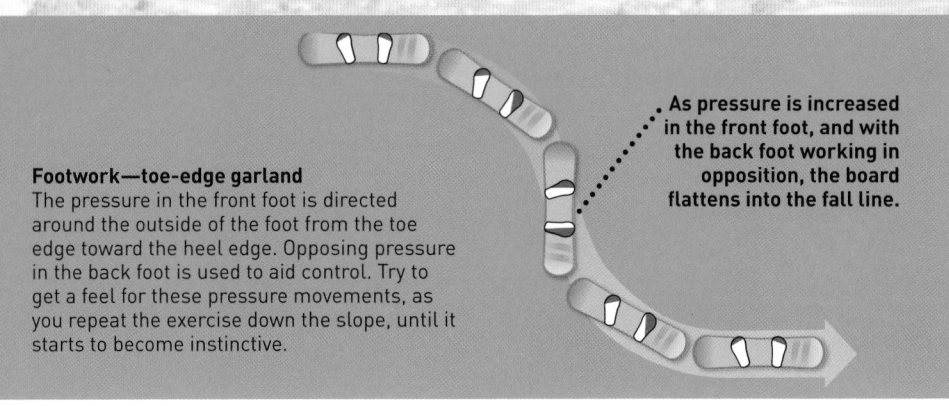

Footwork—toe-edge garland
The pressure in the front foot is directed around the outside of the foot from the toe edge toward the heel edge. Opposing pressure in the back foot is used to aid control. Try to get a feel for these pressure movements, as you repeat the exercise down the slope, until it starts to become instinctive.

As pressure is increased in the front foot, and with the back foot working in opposition, the board flattens into the fall line.

4 Slowly steer the board away from the fall line so that it's pointing across the slope again. Roll the pressure bias back across the front of the board, feeling the progression working in reverse.

5 Return to the side-slip and starting position, before repeating the exercise in the same direction. Keep a relaxed stance and try not to rotate your upper body.

first turn—heel

The basic turn is the final exercise in your learning progression, and introduces the all-important "edge change." Mastering this allows you to change direction by starting the arc on one edge and finishing on the other, riding in the opposite direction.

You already know the necessary techniques to make the perfect basic turn. Run through each step to build your first heel-edge turn, riding from the feet, and with a relaxed upper body.

How not to do it

The heel-edge turn is easily affected by upper-body rotation, which causes a skidded and forced turn. Don't turn your head and shoulders—follow your feet and steer a smooth arc.

1 Heel-edge turn
From a balanced and relaxed stance on your toe edge, press down with your front foot to move into a diagonal side-slip (see pages 74–77).

X

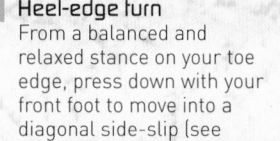

5 Slowly even out the pressure in your feet to return to the side-slip and a stationary position across the slope.

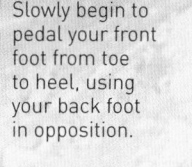

2 Slowly begin to pedal your front foot from toe to heel, using your back foot in opposition.

3 Steer toward the fall line, feeling the front of the board flatten, before moving steering pressure to the heel edge.

4 Steer with your front foot, using opposing pressure in your back foot as you arc back across the slope on your heel edge.

Footwork—heel-edge turn
Here the pressure moves from the toe to heel as the board is steered in an arc. The pressure should be applied through the outside edges of both feet.

As the front foot pressure moves to the new edge, the rear foot is flat to the slope.

first turn—toe

The toe-edge turn is the first time you'll make the transition from heel edge to toe edge. Try to make a smooth, rounded arc, building the turn from your feet step by step, while keeping a relaxed and balanced upper body.

As you progress, try to feel connected with your board, and let your movements flow from the feet up. It's easy to pick up bad habits at this stage, so be strict with yourself to avoid difficulties later on.

The edge change

Feel the front of the board flatten before you move the pressure to the new edge. Don't make the mistake of leaning back. Instead, commit pressure to the outside edge of your front foot, pushing off from the outside edge of your back foot.

3 Steer into the fall line, feeling the front of the board flatten before moving the steering pressure to the toe edge.

Footwork— toe-edge turn
Move pressure around the outside edge of your front foot, as your back foot works in opposition.

········ **Opposing rear foot pressure is essential in order to keep the steering pressure on the front foot.**

Toe-edge turn
From a comfortable, balanced stance pointing across the slope, slowly release your edge tilt to begin a side-slip.

2 Move pressure toward the front of the board to prepare for steering. Slowly pedal from heel to toe with your front foot.

4 Steer with your front foot, using your back foot to hold the pressure forward as you arc back across the slope on your toe edge.

5 Slowly even out the pressure in your feet to return to the side-slip. Come to a stop pointing across the slope.

WATCH IT
see DVD chapter 2

linking and progressing

You now have all the skills required to ride your board around the mountain. From this point on, your snowboarding should be focused toward furthering your understanding of the techniques learned during the basic turn progression. Practice and refine them to suit the varying situations that arise while you are riding your board. The linked basic turn is the first exercise where you can feel the flow of riding—focus on your feet, and cut out unnecessary body movement.

Footwork—linked turns
When riding, notice how you move pressure around the outside edges of your feet to control the nose and tail of the board. This is especially apparent when linking turns.

Back foot pressure is essential in order to keep the steering pressure on the front foot.

As soon as one turn is finished the next begins.

6 As your board turns into the fall line, extend your body, moving your center of gravity over your feet.

7 Steer into the toe-edge turn. Try to feel how the edging, pressure, and steering elements work in every turn.

WATCH IT
see DVD chapter 2

1 Linked turns
Begin from a stationary position on your heel edge.

2 Begin a toe-edge turn, with all the elements of the progression working together.

3 After completing the first turn, instead of coming to a stop, keep sliding, and progress into a heel-edge turn.

4 You can control your speed by making turns right across the slope. Steer more to make a tighter arc and slow down.

5 As you steer across the slope, pay attention to your back foot. Front-foot steering won't work without opposing pressure in the back foot.

8 Finish each turn across the slope, controlling your speed with the line you take.

riding lifts

There are many different types of lifts around to take you to the top of the mountain. Some are more efficient and easier to use than others, but in general, the bigger the lift, the easier and more straightforward it is to use.

Cable cars lead the way in lift efficiency, carrying the most people with the minimum of fuss. Simply take off your board, wait in line with your fellow mountain users, walk into the car, and exit at the top. Cabin lifts typically seat six people and are comfortable, warm, and easy to use. If your board doesn't fit on the rack outside, it's normal to bring it in with you. Chair lifts require you to keep your board on, and actually ride onto and off of the lift. The most technical type of lifts are drag lifts. These are the ones most commonly feared by snowboarders, but drag lifts are easy to use once you know how.

1 **Getting on a drag lift**
Remove your back foot from its binding, placing it just behind your front foot, in a position where you can comfortably stand on both feet.

2 Take hold of the pole with your front hand, pulling it into position between your legs. Keep a solid, balanced stance and prepare for the initial pull as you start to move off.

3 Keep your board straight by aligning it with the lift track. Hold the pole in your front hand, keeping your back hand behind for balance.

How to ride a chair lift

With your back foot free and next to the toe edge, point your board forward. Catch the chair with your back hand, sit, and lower the safety bar. To dismount, lift the bar, and keep your board straight and flat and your hands at your sides. Put your free foot on the middle of the board, stand up, and let the chair move you along. Push clear away, running straight.

1 **Getting off a drag lift**
Wait until you reach the flat, or downhill slope of the arrival area, before letting go of the lift.

2 Dismount by removing the seat from between your legs, making sure you keep the board flat and straight.

3 Release the pole and ride away, steering gently with your front foot. Clear the arrival area as quickly as possible.

go beyond the basics

coming up...

The McNab Pressure Control System: 98—101

Your board is specially designed to turn in a certain way. Here, you will discover how to work your board efficiently and effectively, using the McNab Pressure Control System.

Pressure control: 102—103

Knowing how to flex and bend your board properly is an essential part of achieving a higher level of snowboarding. You will develop your footwork skills, using pressure to turn the board by design, rather than by force.

Adding the edge: 110—115

A smooth and efficient edge change is key to making the perfect carved turn. Here we've set out a series of invaluable exercises to help you hone the accuracy of your edge changes.

Sharper steering: 116—119

As you begin to ride steeper terrain, you'll need to adapt the size of your turn to control your line and speed. You will learn how to make your turns tighter, more dynamic, and more effective, for terrain that's a little more demanding.

introducing the pressure points

To refine your riding technique, you will need to become adept in your use of pressure control, which will allow you to flex and bend the board into more demanding turns. This chapter introduces the "McNab Pressure Control System," which uses four different control points on the board.

The control points are located at either end of the board on your heel and toe edges. As you ride, they are the key to controlling the board as you go into and out of heel- and toe-edge turns. By focusing pressure through these points, you will develop your ability to turn the board by finesse rather than force, and also find your natural way to ride.

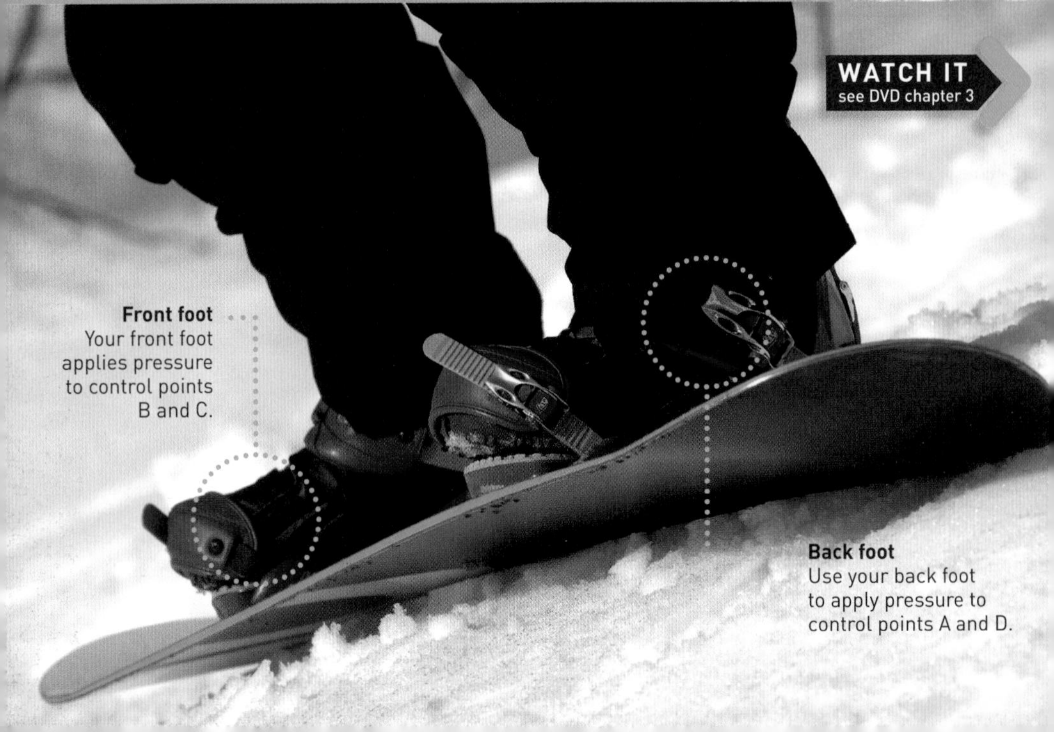

WATCH IT
see DVD chapter 3

Front foot
Your front foot applies pressure to control points B and C.

Back foot
Use your back foot to apply pressure to control points A and D.

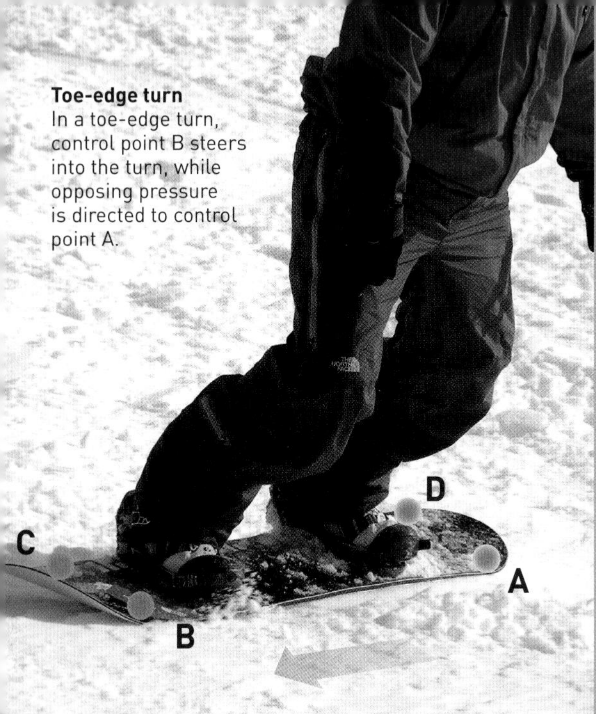

Toe-edge turn
In a toe-edge turn, control point B steers into the turn, while opposing pressure is directed to control point A.

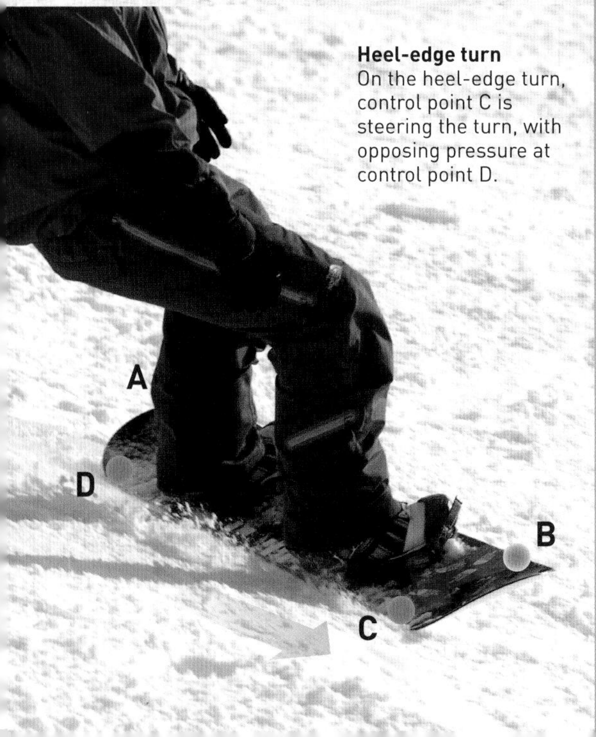

C

D

A

B

Heel-edge turn
On the heel-edge turn, control point C is steering the turn, with opposing pressure at control point D.

A

D

B

C

The control points
For the exercises on the following pages, the control points are labeled A, B, C, and D, and are shown in a graphic of a snowboard being ridden in the goofy stance. If you use a regular stance, simply reverse the control points, so A is still the rear control point on your toe edge.

- **A** is the rear control point on the toe edge.
- **B** is the front control point on the toe edge.
- **C** is the front control point on the heel edge.
- **D** is the rear control point on the heel edge.

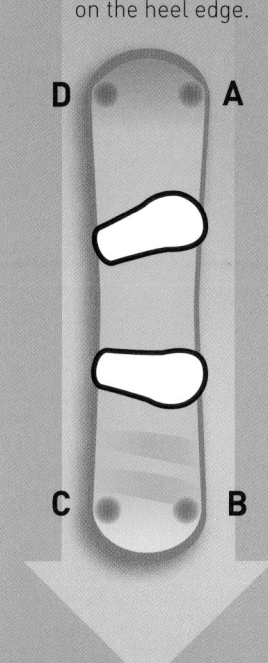

D   A

C   B

working the pressure points

In a carved turn, the board follows a smooth, controlled arc, running along the length of its edge. The flow and shape of this arc are determined by the way in which you apply pressure through the control points, A, B, C and D.

Practice some smooth turns, noticing how your board moves as you prepare, steer and complete each turn. Note the role of the control points, and the sequence they follow.

✓

Carved turn

A carved turn follows a smooth arc, as you turn the board by design rather than force. A carved arc is the most efficient way to change direction. Use skillful foot control to flex and bend the board into the desired arc, using the control points A, B, C, and D.

✗

Skidded turn

A skidded turn uses force and upper-body rotation to turn the board. Weight is moved over the front foot to create a pivot point, on which the hips and shoulders swing the board around, creating a skid. The skidded turn is efficient as a means of stopping or losing speed, but not for general riding purposes.

As steering begins and the edge changes, direct pressure to point C (at the front on the heel edge).

1 Carved turns
Prepare to move the pressure forward into the turn, by feeling for point A (the back control point on the toe edge).

2
To prepare for steering, move pressure forward to point B (the front control point on the toe edge).

4
Control point C steers the turn, while your back foot works in opposition at control point D.

5
Maintain steering pressure at C by increasing opposing pressure at D. The full sequence is A, B, C, D.

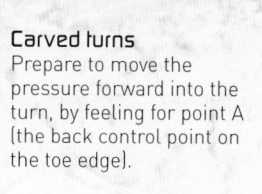

Footwork—carved turn
The foot pressure used in the carved turn is similar to the basic turn. However, it is more refined, with steering and the edge change taking place earlier in the turn.

Pressure is clearly moved toward C for steering

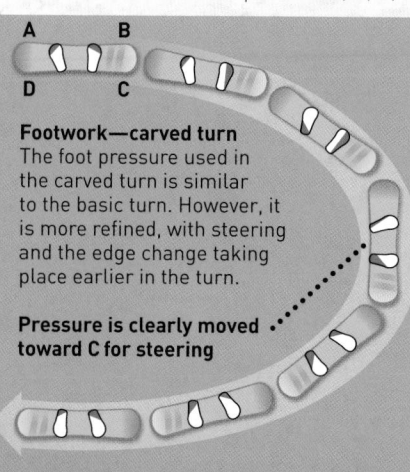

refining pressure transfer

To refine the carved turn, you must become skillful in your manipulation of pressure control. This will enable you to flex and bend the board efficiently and effectively, using the four control points. This exercise will highlight how the board's control points work.

Use your fingers to indicate the movement of pressure around your board during the course of a turn. Point at the control point that you are using as you prepare, steer and execute a turn. Sequence A, B, C, D shown here would be reversed for a toe-edge turn.

1 Controlling pressure

Traveling on your toe edge, prepare to move to your heel edge. This requires pressure transfer to the front of the board. Apply pressure and point to control point A.

2

Point to control point B as you move the pressure to the front of the board in preparation for steering. This is the same pressure movement that you used in the basic progression, prior to steering.

WATCH IT
see DVD chapter 3

3 As you steer into the heel-edge turn, direct the pressure by using your front foot to pedal toward control point C. Point to control point C.

4 As you move onto the heel edge of the board, the opposing pressure in control point D keeps the front foot steering throughout the arc. Point to control point D to highlight this action.

using opposing pressure

You will have noticed that whenever you apply pressure through one foot, there is an opposing pressure in the other foot. It is important to use your feet in opposition to create pressure, rather than moving your weight around. Make sure you keep your hips still and centered.

The exercises here will help you get this feeling of pushing off one foot to pressurize the other, and focus on improving the accuracy of your footwork and steering.

Dry-land exercise
Before you try this exercise on your board, practice the double-pointing exercise without standing on your board. First, create pressure in the outside edges of both feet. Then, transfer the pressure from one foot to the other, noticing how the pressure in each foot works in opposition to the other. With one hand, point at the control point you are using to exert forward pressure. With the other hand, point to the control point on which you are focusing the opposing pressure. Now practice the same exercise strapped onto your board, trying to be as accurate with your pressure movements and pointing as possible.

2 As you steer into the turn, move pressure in your front foot from point C to B. Opposing pressure continues at point D. Keep your back finger pointing to D, and point your front finger to B, on the toe edge.

Double-pointing exercise
Begin by moving presssure from point D to C, pointing your back finger to D, and your front finger to C.

3 Your back foot will follow your front foot onto the toe edge. Continue to steer, with pressure in your front foot remaining at point B. Opposing pressure in your back foot should now be focused toward point A. Move your back finger to point A, keeping your front finger at B.

Footwork—opposing pressure
Here you can see the opposing pressure working in the rear foot to aid the steering pressure in the front foot.

Steering pressure moves toward control point C, with opposing pressure coming from control point D.

WATCH IT
see DVD chapter 3

building pressure control

Riding with your hands on your knees is a great exercise to give you improved steering control by helping to focus on the movements of your feet, eliminate any unwanted upper-body influence, and utilize opposing pressure. Without the influence of any upper-body movements, you'll have to overemphasize your use of pressure and steering to control the board and make the turn.

Hands-on-knees exercise

Place your hands on the inside edges of your knees. Keep your legs flexed and be strict with yourself, controlling the board only from your knees down. As you work your feet through the pressure-transfer control points A, B, C, and D, notice how your knees mirror the tiny movements of your feet. As a result of this, your hands should move, too.

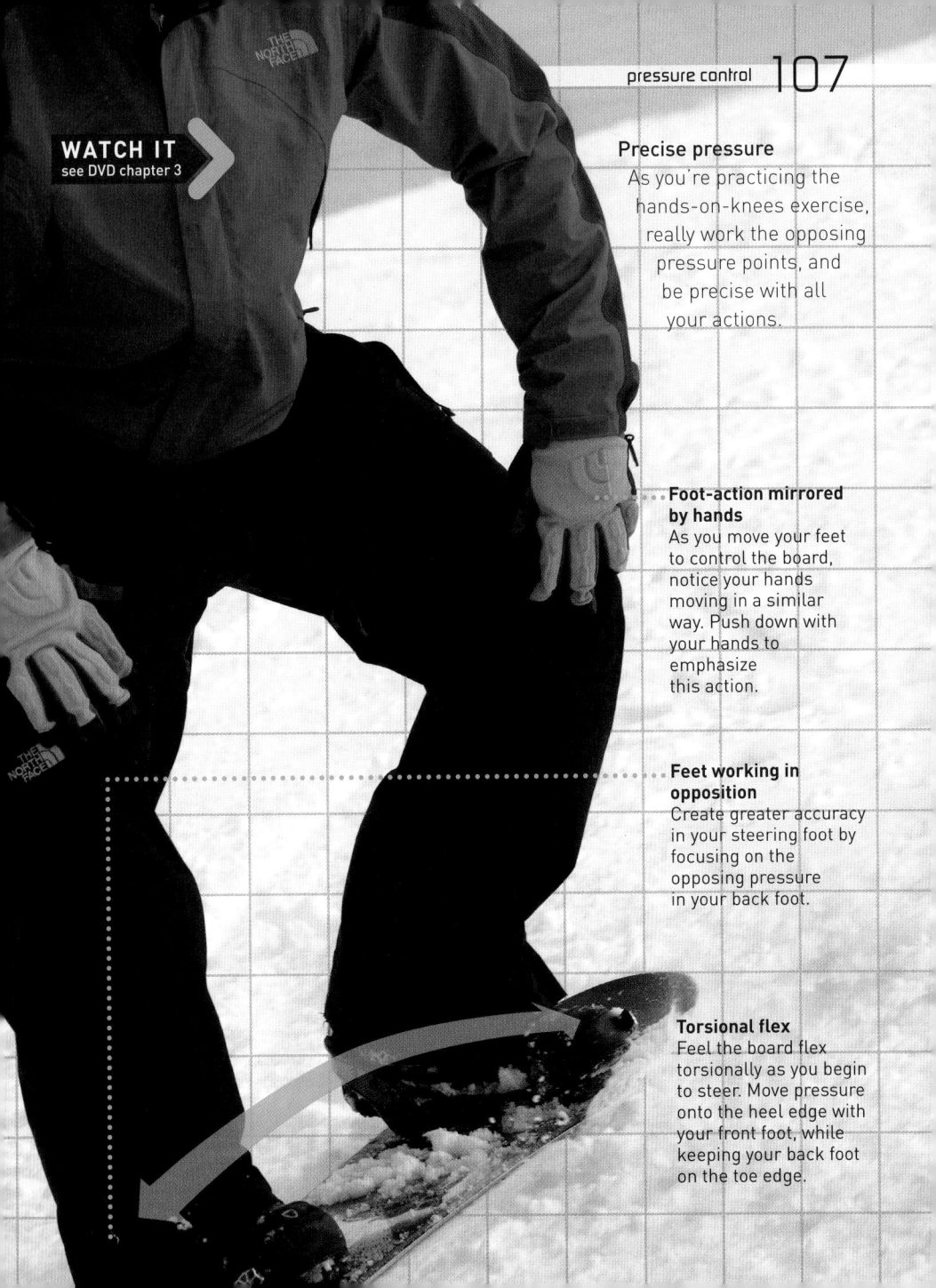

WATCH IT
see DVD chapter 3 >

Precise pressure
As you're practicing the hands-on-knees exercise, really work the opposing pressure points, and be precise with all your actions.

Foot-action mirrored by hands
As you move your feet to control the board, notice your hands moving in a similar way. Push down with your hands to emphasize this action.

Feet working in opposition
Create greater accuracy in your steering foot by focusing on the opposing pressure in your back foot.

Torsional flex
Feel the board flex torsionally as you begin to steer. Move pressure onto the heel edge with your front foot, while keeping your back foot on the toe edge.

wait, don't rotate

This exercise is used to develop smoother steering control and a more accurate movement toward the new edge. It can help eliminate excessive upper body rotation, and increase your awareness of the control points during the initiation phase of the turn.

Follow the normal sequence for your turn, starting at control point A, and moving pressure through B and C, using control point D to finish the turn. At each stage, pause just before steering begins, shown here at control point B. Initially, hold this pause for a count of three, before steering slowly into the turn. As you improve, reduce the pause to a count of two, and finally one, while trying to turn with the same accuracy each time.

1 **Holding point B**
Move pressure forward from control point A, to control point B, applying opposing pressure in B.

2 Hold the pressure at point B for a count of two, feeling the opposing pressure at point A, at the rear of the board.

3 Hold the pressure at point B for a count of three, before slowly steering into the new turn at control point C.

How not to do it

The majority of snowboarders initiate their turns using their shoulders and hip. This technique, although not wrong, causes the board to over-rotate, producing a forced, skidded turn. This disrupts the basic stance, as shown here. This exercise should help eliminate upper-body influence, and produce a smoother, rounder turn.

4 The pressure moves slowly across to point C for a smooth edge change, and the turn begins to happen.

5 Steering pressure at point C steers the turn, while opposing pressure is applied to point D at the rear of the board, to assist the steering movement at the front of the board.

WATCH IT
see DVD chapter 3

precise steering

After practicing the preparation for steering in the previous exercise, now you can take it one step further and develop your accuracy in actually steering to the new edge. In this exercise, you slow down the pedaling movement between B and C, or C and B—this gives you greater accuracy when initiating the turn.

Opposing pressure

In this exercise, you are going to steer the board with a gentle transfer of pressure, rather than trying to force the board around with rotation. Create strong opposing pressure in the outside edges of both feet, move the pressure forward, and slowly begin to steer, feeling your front foot rolling the board across to the new edge. In this toe-edge turn, strong pressure at control point D is used to control the steering from C toward B.

1 Precise steering

For this toe-edge turn, the pressure-control sequence will be D, C, B, A. Using the outside edge of your back foot, drive pressure forward from control point D to point C, in preparation for the turn. Hold the pressure here as you did in the previous exercise.

2

Slowly steer from control point C to control point B. Feel your front foot rolling the board as it goes flat, and then toward the new edge at point B. Keep the opposing pressure in point D working to control this movement.

3

Drive the pressure through control point B, flexing the board to steer into the new turn. Your back foot will now follow to the new edge, moving the pressure to control point A in order to keep steering pressure at point B throughout the turn.

edging and balance

As your steering becomes more precise, you'll begin to notice the feel of your front foot rolling the board flat in between each turn. This flattening of the board is essential—the new turn cannot begin until this point is reached.

Begin to focus on the moment when one turn has finished and the other has not yet begun. Treat this moment between turns as a moment of stillness, a return to center. It is the one point in your turns where you don't have to work for balance, so relax!

The upper body is upright but relaxed

Center of gravity is balanced over the feet

The board flattens as it moves from one edge to the other

Standing up

In everyday life, when your feet are flat on the floor, you normally maintain a relaxed upright position in which the frame of your body is aligned, and you can balance without undue muscle tension. Similarly, at the point between turns, when you feel your front foot flatten to the slope, you can stand up and let your body relax in a comfortable, balanced position. Stretch out your frame, and let your feet do the work.

Extending and flexing
Stand up on the board to balance between turns. This returns you to a neutral position from which you can flex as the edge tilt increases in the next turn.

Stand tall
By standing tall when your board is flat, you bring your center of gravity over your feet for balance.

Stand small
In the turn, you have to flex over the edge, tensing your muscles to maintain a balanced position on the board.

Once the turn has begun, flex to stay balanced. Return to an upright position as you move out of the turn.

It is now time to test your snowboarding ability, and also learn a new and valuable skill. Riding fakie (backward) will help you to understand the importance of the pressure movements you have been mastering. With practice, you will feel as comfortable riding fakie as you do riding forward.

riding fakie

1

How to ride fakie
Turn your head toward the tail of the board, and adopt a normal stance. Your back foot has now become your front foot.

2

Move the pressure forward, toward the outside edge of your new front foot, and the tail of the board. Use your new back foot in opposition.

3

Extend your body to balance. As your front foot flattens to the slope, your back foot continues to work in opposition.

Snowboard design

Most snowboards are designed so they can be ridden both backward and forward. Riding fakie is also known as riding "switch," because you have simply switched around the way you ride.

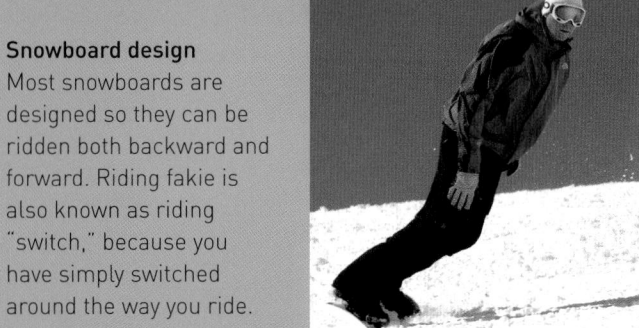

4 Begin to steer, pedaling the pressure slowly across the board. Transfer the pressure onto the toe edge to steer into the turn, remembering not to rotate your upper body.

5 Steer the turn with your front foot, moving the pressure forward. Your back foot works in opposition to torsionally flex the board through the turn.

WATCH IT
see DVD chapter 3

short-rad funnel

As you progress to steeper terrain, you'll need to make a tighter arc to control your speed efficiently.

To steer a tighter arc, you must flex and bend the board more strongly into the turn. Your pressure, steering and edge-control movements will have to be more dynamic and effective. Practicing the funnel method will help you make shorter-radius turns, as you speed up your control movements to naturally tighten your arcs.

Speed control
You can control your speed by following a tighter line, and making tighter finishes to your turns.

Count of one
Match your forward movement (D to C) to a count of one, increasing the steering pressure to B once again, to further tighten the arc.

Steering and pressure
By speeding up the pressure movements between the rear and front control points, you will shorten the space between turns, while increasing the amount of pressure you transfer forward. Start with a count of three, then a count of two, then one, finally linking your turns, one after the other.

The funnel method
As the control movements between your turns speed up, your turns will become tighter and closer together, giving the exercise its funnel shape and name.

Count of three
Start with a count of three between D and C, before applying strong steering pressure at B.

Count of two
Speed up your forward pressure movement (A to B) to a count of two, increasing the amount of pressure for steering at C, to flex the board into a tighter arc.

Radius
A shorter radius doesn't mean a faster turn.

Continual turns
Move straight from the end of one turn into the beginning of the next, flowing with a continual, dynamic movement.

WATCH IT
see DVD chapter 3

the corridor

The corridor is a great exercise for practicing short-radius turns. Here you choose a narrow corridor of slope and try to stay within its confines as you descend.

Make your movements dynamic, smooth, and effective. Concentrate on making strong pressure movements between control points A and B for effective steering into the turn. Finish each turn off to control your speed, before moving into the next one.

Turn by design
Don't force the board around.

Test yourself

Make your corridor narrower and use steeper terrain as you progress to test your skills. Control your speed by the line you take, and turn by design, not force.

Keep your upper body still and relaxed

Emphasize the steering in your feet by mirroring it with your knees

Keep practicing

Steering plays a very important role in short-radius turns. Try the corridor exercise with your hands on your knees to really get your feet working, and increase how much you work your board (see pages 106–107). Make sure you concentrate on the opposing pressure as you bend the front of the board into each new turn.

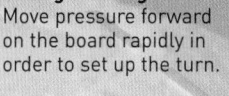

Strong steering
Move pressure forward
on the board rapidly in
order to set up the turn.

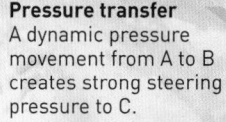

Pressure transfer
A dynamic pressure
movement from A to B
creates strong steering
pressure to C.

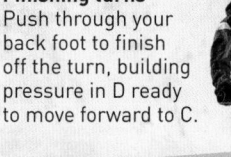

Finishing turns
Push through your
back foot to finish
off the turn, building
pressure in D ready
to move forward to C.

Flowing movement
Let your movements
flow. You should begin
to feel the sequence
working naturally.

WATCH IT
see DVD chapter 3

go further

coming up...

Terrain and conditions: 124–137

As your technique improves, you will be able to take on greater challenges, such as steeper slopes, variable terrain, and changing snow conditions. In this chapter, you will develop your riding skills further, to suit the natural terrain of the mountain.

Freestyle: 138–145

It won't be long before you're looking for natural shapes to launch off, rather than ride around. With a multitude of spins and grabs, freestyle is one of snowboarding's most exhilarating and visually exciting disciplines. Once you've mastered the basic moves, the sky is, quite literally, the limit.

Freeriding: 146–151

Freeriding brings together all the skills and techniques of snowboarding, allowing you the freedom to explore the most exciting terrain the mountain has to offer. With freeriding, you can test your technical ability, display your freestyle prowess, and develop your personal expression. You will learn how to match your own movements to the terrain of the mountain.

variable terrain

Once you are confident on easy and moderately angled slopes, you can start to increase the difficulty of the task in front of you simply by tackling steeper and more variable terrain. As the slope changes, you need to modify your line and your movements accordingly, to ride in control with the mountain. Control your speed through the line you take, look ahead, and don't get caught out.

Arced turns
Plan your route, making flowing arcs that work with the terrain. You may need to make sharper turns in one direction to counteract a sideways gradient across the piste.

Direction of travel
The direction in which you want to travel will not always match the path you have to take. Look at how the slope is changing and choose the best line to suit the terrain.

Keep a relaxed and open stance
Be strong and active with your feet to steer, but relaxed with your legs and body to balance, and absorb bumps. An open stance gives you a good view of the terrain ahead.

Complete turns
Ensuring that you complete each turn controls your speed, and helps you create a platform for the coming turn. A strong finish on one turn can really help you start the next.

a

b

WATCH IT
see DVD chapter 4

speed awareness

When you are feeling confident on shallow variable terrain, you can increase the difficulty of the task simply by increasing the angle of the slope. Steep terrain is one of the more demanding aspects of snowboarding.

The turns that you have practiced up to this point are called cross-over turns. Cross-over turns have a relatively gentle edge change and steering initiation phase, which can cause an increase in speed toward the fall line. As you progress to steeper terrain, be prepared for this sudden acceleration during the transition phase of the turn.

Flattening the board

In a cross-over turn, the board has to be flattened before the new turn can begin. The body moves from one edge, over the board, and onto the other edge as the new turn begins. The control elements of edging, pressure, and steering begin relatively gently, and increase in force as the turn develops. This gentle turn initiation period means that on steep terrain, the board can accelerate quite rapidly toward the fall line before you can control your speed by steering across the slope. For more control on steeper slopes, it may be better to use the cross-under turn technique, which dispenses with this transitional phase (see pages 128–131).

1
The cross-over turn
At the end of the heel turn, your body is angled to the inside of the turn, balanced over your heel edge.

2
Move into the toe-edge turn by flattening the board to the slope. Move your body up and over the flat board for balance.

3
As you start the toe-edge turn your body crosses over the board to the toe edge. Your speed may increase towards the fall line.

Heel edge
The line in the snow shows the board coming into the turn on its heel edge.

Transition
As the board changes edges, it briefly flattens to the snow.

WATCH IT
see DVD chapter 4

Toe edge
With the edge change complete, the board moves off on its toe edge.

Increased speed
On steeper terrain, the gentle nature of the cross-over turn results in an increase in speed as the board moves towards the fall line.

speed control—the theory

For effective speed management on steep terrain, you need to drive the board around the turn without a rapid increase in speed. With its pronounced acceleration phase, the cross-over turn isn't ideally suited to this task, so a new technique, the cross-under turn, must now be learned.

The cross-under edge change is very effective on steep terrain, because the turn initiation is performed with the board steered up the hill, and so edging, steering, and pressure can be very powerful in the early phase of this dynamic turn.

1 The cross-under turn— the theory
At the end of a heel-edge turn, your body is angled to the inside of the turn, balanced over the heel edge, much as it would be for a cross-over turn.

2 Instead of moving your body over the board, you steer the board up the slope, so it crosses under the body.

3 The pressure moves directly from the back heel edge to the front toe edge. Pressure release from the back of the board sometimes causes it to leave the ground.

Heel edge
The line in the snow shows the board coming into the turn on its heel edge.

No transition
The cross-under turn dispenses with the transitional phase.

Toe edge
With the edge change complete, the new turn can begin immediately.

Edge change
With no transition phase, the cross-under turn allows you to steer straight onto the new edge.

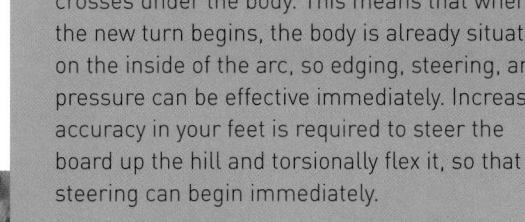

4 The board is now steered powerfully onto the front control point to initiate the turn. The board has crossed under the body, the body is already balanced to the inside of the new turn which has begun without any acceleration toward the fall line.

Steer immediately

In the cross-under edge change, the board crosses under the body. This means that when the new turn begins, the body is already situated on the inside of the arc, so edging, steering, and pressure can be effective immediately. Increased accuracy in your feet is required to steer the board up the hill and torsionally flex it, so that steering can begin immediately.

speed control—the practice

The cross-under edge change uses dynamic movements to initiate the pressure and steering movement earlier in the turn, thus creating the potential for a tighter arc and less acceleration toward the fall line. This is an advanced technical maneuver and, as before, the board turns through skillful manipulation and by design rather than force.

The cross-over edge change follows the pressure sequence A, B, C, and D. The cross-under edge change sequence changes slightly. Start on A, pull up on B, apply strong pressure and steering to C, and finish with strong opposing pressure to D.

1 Performing a cross-under turn
Having finished a heel edge turn, use precise movements in your feet to drive pressure back strongly to control point D. Begin to pull up on control point C.

2
Pull up on control point C, steering the board up the slope so that it crosses under your body.

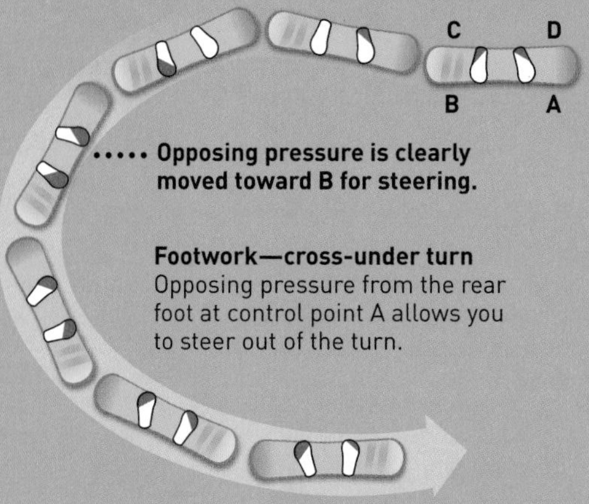

C D

B A

····· **Opposing pressure is clearly moved toward B for steering.**

Footwork—cross-under turn
Opposing pressure from the rear foot at control point A allows you to steer out of the turn.

The cross-under turn is very effective in variable terrain, where control of speed and line is extremely important.

3 Torsionally flex the board, driving the pressure accurately toward control point B, for immediate, strong steering on the new edge. Don't rotate the board, as this will cause skidding. You are now on the inside of the new turning arc.

4 Control the pressure and steering at B by applying strong opposing pressure with your rear foot to control point A.

WATCH IT see DVD chapter 4

variable conditions

The conditions on the mountain are constantly changing. Deep snow, icy snow, bumpy terrain, flat light, and white-out conditions are just some of the variables for which you'll need to be able to adapt your riding style. Sometimes you'll need to be able to adapt to all these different conditions within the same day, so always be aware and ready to change your riding at a moment's notice.

a

b

c

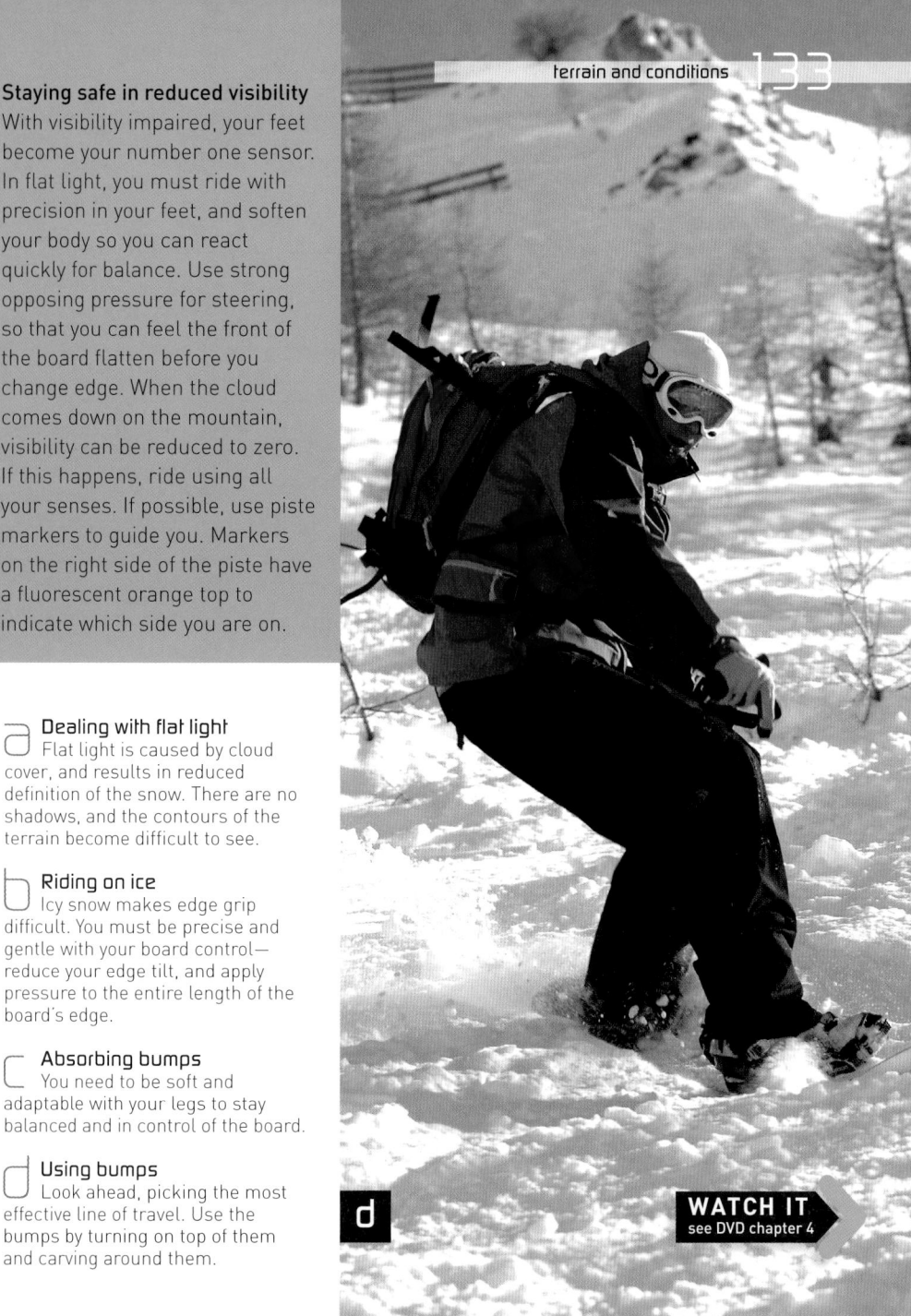

Staying safe in reduced visibility

With visibility impaired, your feet become your number one sensor. In flat light, you must ride with precision in your feet, and soften your body so you can react quickly for balance. Use strong opposing pressure for steering, so that you can feel the front of the board flatten before you change edge. When the cloud comes down on the mountain, visibility can be reduced to zero. If this happens, ride using all your senses. If possible, use piste markers to guide you. Markers on the right side of the piste have a fluorescent orange top to indicate which side you are on.

a Dealing with flat light

Flat light is caused by cloud cover, and results in reduced definition of the snow. There are no shadows, and the contours of the terrain become difficult to see.

b Riding on ice

Icy snow makes edge grip difficult. You must be precise and gentle with your board control— reduce your edge tilt, and apply pressure to the entire length of the board's edge.

c Absorbing bumps

You need to be soft and adaptable with your legs to stay balanced and in control of the board.

d Using bumps

Look ahead, picking the most effective line of travel. Use the bumps by turning on top of them and carving around them.

d

WATCH IT
see DVD chapter 4

riding powder

Cutting deep, fresh turns through untracked powder is every snowboarder's dream and is one of the greatest feelings you can experience on a board. While it looks effortless, your first forays into the steep and deep may tell a different story.

Make clean arcs
You cannot skid to control your speed in powder, so keep your speed under control by making clean, well-finished arcs. Look ahead, and plan your line.

WATCH IT
see DVD chapter 4

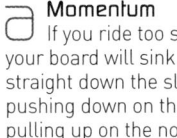

Momentum
If you ride too slowly, your board will sink. Ride straight down the slope, pushing down on the tail and pulling up on the nose until the board starts to "float" across the slope. This is your minimum cruising speed.

Steering
As with normal riding, steering in powder is all about applying pressure to the right control point on the board. As your momentum increases, you will start to feel the pressure build under your front foot. You will be able to steer as normal, but with less effort.

Balancing
As the whole base of the board is in contact with the snow, you can keep your center of gravity over the middle of your feet, rather than over the toe or heel edges. This makes balancing much easier, and you can generally stand a bit taller when riding powder.

Pressure
Using the whole base of the board means you have more surface area to push through. This also means there is more snow pushing back, so the amount of pressure needed for each turn is greater. You can really bend and flex your board into and out of each turn.

powder techniques

To ride on powder, you will be able to use the basic snowboarding techniques you have already learned, with a few modifications for the terrain.

A turn on powder requires a greater application of pressure because the board grips the slope more sharply. The challenge is to keep the nose slightly up and the tail down, allowing the board to plane. It's especially important to apply pressure to the control points, rather than leaning your weight back.

1 Riding on powder
Push backward through your back foot, and run straight until you feel the pressure build under your front foot.

2 For a toe-edge turn, transfer the pressure and steering toward control point C, now just in front of your front foot.

3 Transfer pressure into the turn delicately. You will have to carefully judge how much forward pressure is needed for steering.

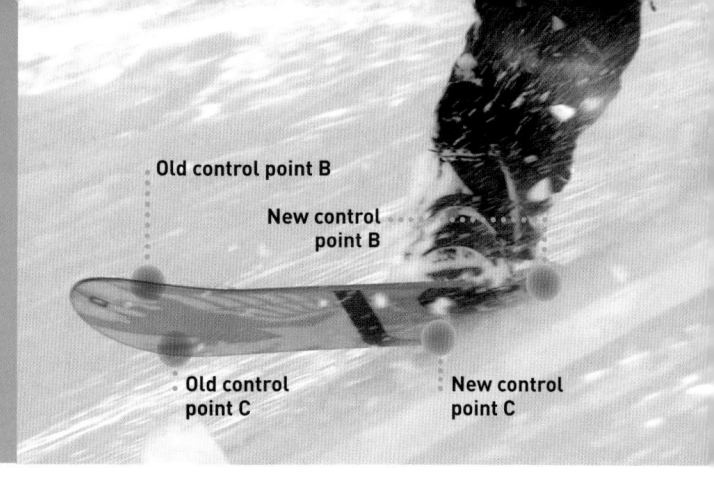

Pressure points for powder

The pressure-control sequence is the same as for a normal turn, but with the nose raised, the front contact points B and C move down the edge, closer to the front foot. This means you don't need to move steering pressure as far forward.

Old control point B

New control point B

Old control point C

New control point C

4 Steer through the front foot, using strong pressure in the back foot to bend the board into the arc.

5 Finish the arc by bending the tail, using strong back-foot pressure, pushing straight down through the board.

introducing freestyle

Freestyle snowboarding has always been influenced by skateboarding, and most skateboarding-style tricks have found their way onto the mountain in some form or other. As you progress, the mountain terrain will start to resemble a huge skate park, and it won't be long before you find yourself looking for terrain shapes to launch off, rather than ride around.

Freestyle tips

There are many things to jump and drop off around the mountain, but not all of them are suitable for you to ride off. Here are a few tips to soften the landings, and help you ride safely:

- Make sure that what you jump off has a good landing area. Look before you leap—be sure you know what you'll be landing on, and that it's clear.
- Good foundations are the key to progress, so take things slowly and master the smaller jumps first.
- Always wear protective clothing suitable for freestyle riding, and never ride alone.
- If you're riding in a snowboard park, adhere to the park rules, and be courteous to other users.

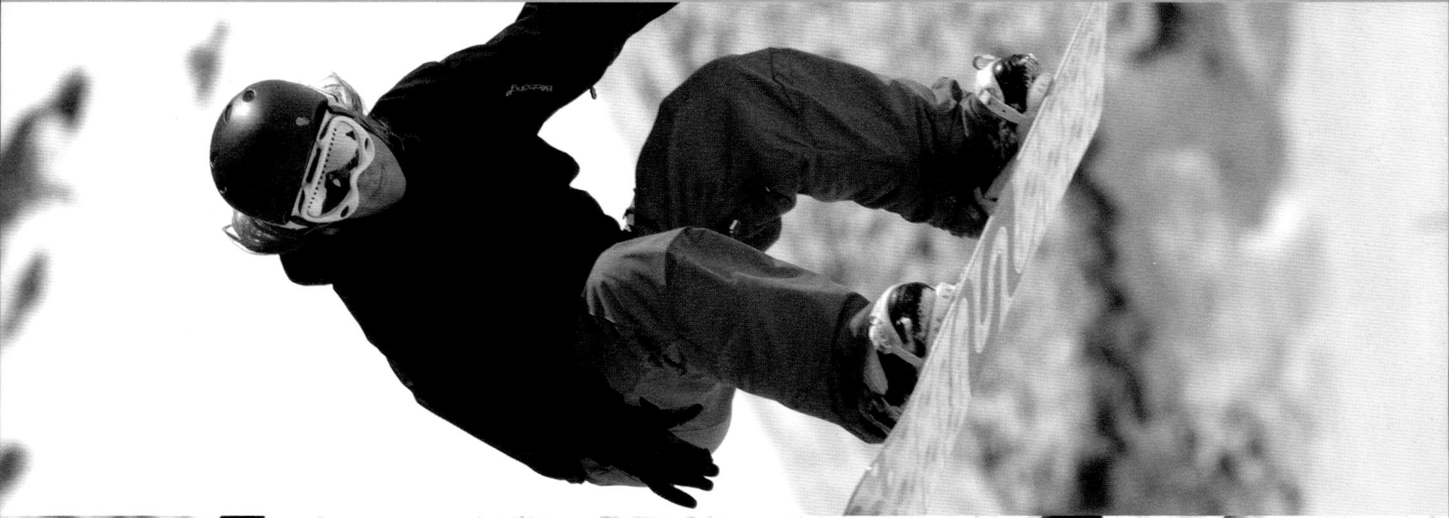

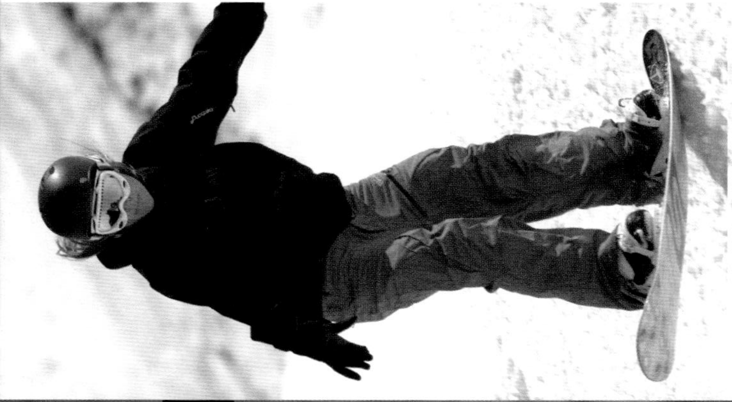

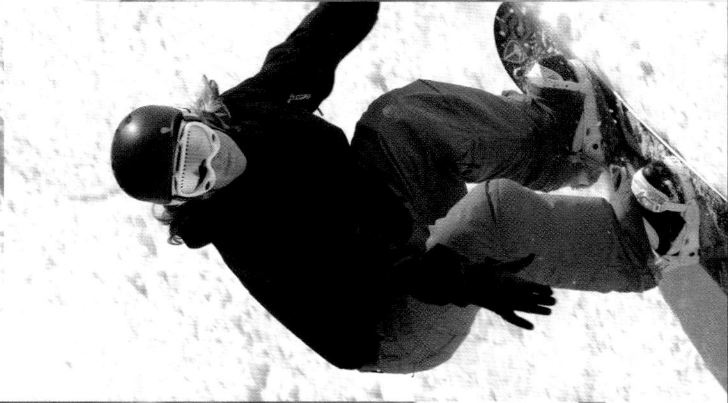

ollies

The ollie, a trick derived from skateboarding, is a key skill for freestyle development. The ollie allows you to spring into the air off flat surfaces, introduces you to the feeling of being airborne, and means you can leap higher off jumps without having to increase your speed.

The ollie uses the flex properties of your board to spring you into the air. A movement of pressure, from the nose of the board to the tail, strongly flexes the back of the board, creating a rebound effect that propels you into the air.

1 Ollieing
From a straight run on gentle terrain, exert pressure with your front foot, and prepare to spring off the tail of the board. Sink low so that you're ready to "pop," or spring, into the air.

2
Drive the pressure to the back of the board in one swift movement, pushing from your front foot to the outside edge of your back foot, and then toward the tail.

3
Pull up strongly on your front foot to flex the board. Spring off the tail and leap into the air.

4 Lead with your front foot, driving it upward and forward to flatten out the board. Pull your knees up and apart, for extra height and float.

5 Land on both feet simultaneously, with your board flat to the snow. Keep your body flexed and relaxed.

6 Absorb the impact of landing with your legs, and ride away in a straight line. As you become more confident, look for bumps in the terrain to help you pop up.

WATCH IT
see DVD chapter 5

kickers

Most freestyle maneuvers require a little more time in the air than the ollie can offer. Now you need to use your newly acquired skills on terrain that will help you increase your lift, and air time. A kicker is a specially shaped snowboard jump with a take off and landing, as found in most terrain parks.

The technique for riding kickers is very similar to the basic technique for the ollie. On a kicker, the curved shape, called a transition, provides most of the lift. This means that the ollie action can be less dramatic, so start with small jumps and build up slowly.

1 **Riding a kicker** Ride in with enough speed to reach your landing area. Stay relaxed and flexed, with your board flat to the snow.

2 As you reach the kicker, slowly extend, using the same pressure movement as for the ollie, springing softly off the tail.

3 Pop gently off the tail of the board, keeping your hips and shoulders in line with the board. Keep your eyes on the landing area.

4 Pull your feet up, and push your knees apart for extra height and float in an arc.

WATCH IT
see DVD chapter 5

5 As you begin to drop back down to the ground, extend your legs slightly toward the landing area, and prepare to land.

6 Make sure that you land with your board flat to the snow, and straight. Flex your legs to absorb the impact of landing.

7 Ride away in a straight line, before turning to control your speed.

grabs

Once you have mastered jumping off kickers, you can add some style to your air tricks by grabbing your board. There are many different types of grab to choose from, most of which have, like the ollie, derived from skateboarding. Grabbing and tweaking (manipulating) your board is what freestyle riding is all about.

The key areas of the board to be grabbed are the nose and tail, and the toe and heel edges between your feet. There's more to grabbing your board than just holding on to the edge—try to tweak your board and your body against the grab and add some personal style to the trick.

a

a Stale fish grab
The strangely named stale fish grab is particularly stylish. Grab your heel edge between your feet with your back hand.

b Mute grab
To perform a mute grab, use your front hand to grab the toe edge of your board between your feet.

c Tail grab
The tail grab is quite simple, but also visually impressive. Use your back hand to grab the tail and tweak.

d Indy grab
The indy is one of the most popular and stylish grabs, and the one that you should master first. Your rear hand grabs the toe edge of the board, in front of your rear foot.

WATCH IT
see DVD chapter 5

b

c
d

introducing freeriding

Freeriding is the finest of snowboarding's arts. It begins when you are no longer concerned about simply getting from the top of the mountain to the bottom, but about the way you make your journey. Freeriding requires you to look at the mountain as a whole, and not just as a series of groomed and graded pistes. Freeriding will lead you away from this regulated environment, and toward the greater challenges that lie just beyond.

Making the most of the mountain

As you start to demand more from your riding, you will also begin to demand more from the terrain that you ride. Your journey is now well underway, and you are on the never-ending search for the perfect ride.

Freeriding is about matching your movements to the mountain terrain. It is about flowing with the mountain, and exploring the endless possibilities, such as carving and jumping, that await on every descent.

Search for the mountain's natural lines. Look for the perfectly sculpted terrain shapes, the drops, the chutes, and the rollers, and incorporate them all into a creative descent.

freeriding—tips

Your search for the mountain's hidden treasures may take you out into the untamed, untracked, natural terrain, found off the piste and in the backcountry. The backcountry of the high mountains is a truly inspirational place, but it does pose serious challenges. To ride here safely, you will need to call on your most advanced techniques, as well as learning some all-important mountain safety skills.

Safety

You must be aware of the natural dangers posed by the unpatrolled mountain. Here are some important tips to help you on your way:

- Learn to assess the snowpack, in order to gauge the avalanche risk posed by the slopes.
- Carry tools and safety equipment such as an avalanche transceiver, probe, and a shovel.
- Don't go anywhere unless you're sure of the risks involved.
- Don't follow the tracks of others unless you know the area.
- Never ride alone, and be responsible for your actions.

freeriding techniques

Freeriding incorporates every aspect of snowboarding, taking the big air from the park, the flat land tricks and carving techniques from the piste, and the deep powerful turns from the powder. You now have everything at your fingertips, and it's about you, your skills, and the mountain.

Try to match your movements to the terrain you're riding, look ahead, and be adaptable to change as you go. Try to play with the terrain, explore your techniques, and enjoy yourself. Increase your use of pressure through each of the control points—you'll make more dynamic turns, and have greater control over your line and speed.

Combining skills

Freeriding is a different skill to riding on the piste, so bear these suggestions in mind:

- Power through the ends of turns by increasing your pressure to control points A and D. This will bend the back of the board into a tighter arc and help you move into the new turn

- When riding off drops, make sure you know exactly what is below you. The landing should suit the height of the jump, and the speed at which you'll land.

- Land from a jump with your board flat and straight—absorb the impact with your legs. If the snow is deep, keep the pressure slightly back, so that the nose doesn't sink and dive.

boarding on the net

Listed below is a small selection of snowboarding websites from around the world, containing everything from gear reviews, latest news, and articles, to governing bodies, and snowboard vacation operators.

US and CANADA resources

www.usasa.org
The official website of the United States of America Snowboard Association.

www.csf.ca
The site of the Canadian Snowboard Federation, with information on events and coaching.

www.snowcanada.com
The complete guide to skiing and snowboarding in western Canada.

www.snowboard.com
A web community for snowboarders, containing trick tips, resort information, and reviews.

www.snowboardermag.com
The website of US magazine Snowboarder, containing features, videos, and photos.

AUSTRALIA and NEW ZEALAND resources

www.skiingaustralia.org.au
The site of Ski and Snowboard Australia, the governing body for competitive snowsports in Australia.

www.snow.co.nz
New Zealand's leading ski and snowboard website, with daily snow reports.

UK and IRELAND resources

www.snowboardclub.co.uk
The UK's biggest snowboard information site, catering to all your snowboarding needs.

www.soulsports.co.uk
Profiles and news from the UK's leading snowboarders.

www.snowsportgb.com
The national governing body for wintersports in the UK, Snowsports GB runs the UK's national snowboard team.

www.snowlife.org.uk
A site designed for newcomers to the sport, including everything you need to know about starting out in snowboarding.

www.mcnabsnowboarding.com
The UK's leading freeride, freestyle, and backcountry snowboard specialists, providing courses, clinics, and training camps for all levels of riders.

www.docsnow.co.uk
The website for the UK snowboarding magazine, with reviews and information on equipment, resorts, and events.

www.snowboard-asylum.com
The UK's leading online snowboard store.

board talk

Avalanche kit—a shovel, probe, and transceiver, carried when riding off-piste.

Backcountry—the untamed areas of the mountain, beyond the boundaries of the ski area.

Backside turn—a heel-edge turn.

Base—the flat surface under the board, made from a polyethylene-based material.

Basic turn—a turn that allows the rider to change direction by steering into the fall line and performing an edge change.

Carve—a rounded turn, where the board runs along its edge, from nose to tail.

Control point—a specific point on the board, used for pressure control when turning.

Cross-over turn—a turn where the rider's body moves over the board during the transition phase of the turn.

Cross-under turn—a turn where the rider steers the board up the hill so it crosses under the body, often causing the board to leave the ground.

Diagonal side-slip—similar to the side-slip, but with a pressure movement applied to one end of the board to skid diagonally down the slope.

Drag lift—a lift that tows you up the hill.

Edge—the metal strip that runs along either side of the board. See also: rail.

Edge change—the point in a turn where a rider crosses from one edge to the other, also known as the transition phase.

Edging—to tilt the board onto its heel or toe edge. Along with pressure and steering, one of the three key elements of snowboarding.

Fakie—to ride backward. See also: switch.

Falling leaf—a basic exercise where the rider progresses downhill by moving back and forth across the slope.

Fall line—the straightest route down a slope, as dictated by gravity.

Freeride—to ride the mountain by using every aspect of snowboarding technique.

Freestyle—to perform stunts and maneuvers while riding a snowboard.

Frontside turn—a toe-edge turn.

Fundamental elements—the three essential controlling elements of snowboarding—steering, pressure and edging.

Garland—an exercise that involves steering into the fall line to simulate the initiation phase of a turn, without performing a complete turn.

Goofy—to ride with the right foot forward.

Grab—an aerial maneuver where the edge of the board is grabbed for style and balance.

Heel edge—the edge located under the heels.

High back—the rear support spoiler on a snowboard binding.

Kicker—a specially designed jump, as found in a snow park.

Longitudinal flex—where the board is bent upward along its length.

Mini tool—a small, easily carried, and specially designed screwdriver for adjusting bindings.

Off-piste—anywhere on the mountain beyond the marked ski area.

Ollie—a freestyle trick to get air off flat ground.

Piste—a marked, groomed trail on the mountain.

Powder skirt—a powder gaiter found inside some jackets to stop snow from getting in.

Pressure—to control the board by applying pressure through the feet. Along with edging and steering, one of the three key elements of snowboarding.

Pressure bias—when the pressure is concentrated in one spot, more than another.

Rail—another word for the edge, more commonly used in the US than elsewhere.

Railslide—a trick in which the board slides on a metal rail or similar object.

Recommended stance—the stance recommended by the board manufacturer, which can be customized to suit your riding style.

Regular—to ride with the left foot forward.

Sidecut—the curved shape of the board's edge, specially designed so the board turns as it runs along its edge.

Side-slip—a controlled sideways skid down the slope, perpendicular to the fall line.

Steering—to steer a path by torsionally flexing the board. Along with edging and pressure, one of the three ket elements of snowboarding.

Straight running—a basic exercise, practiced on very gentle slopes, where the rider moves forward in a straight line.

Switch—to ride backward, the same as fakie.

Toe edge—the edge located under the toes.

Torsional flex—where the board is twisted along its length, as in steering.

Transceiver—a transmitter and receiver used in avalanche emergencies.

Tweak—where the board is bent and flexed in the air using either the feet or a grab.

PISTE GRADINGS

US, Canada, Australia, New Zealand	Europe	Level of difficulty
●	▬	Typically a wide, shallow, groomed, beginner slope.
	▬	An easy slope, slightly steeper or narrower than a beginner run.
■	▬	An intermediate slope that is usually groomed.
◆	▬	An advanced slope, often ungroomed, ranging from terrain that is just beyond intermediate level, to expert terrain such as steep chutes and drops.
◆◆		

index

A

accidents, assisting at 28, 29
altitude 27
ankle gaiters 47
arced turns 124, 131, 134, 151
arm position 59
avalanche 148
    safety gear 36, 37

B

back protectors 36
backward, riding 38, 40,
    114–115
balance
    and boots 44
    center of gravity 22, 25, 58,
        61, 90
    and edging 112–113
    and eyeline 59
    and movement, see: stances
    over bumps 133
    in powder snow 135
    standing up 61
    and turning 24
beginners
    board for 40
    falling down 60–61
    practice terrain 78
bindings 34, 37, 38, 44
    angles 42, 54, 55
    disks 42, 55
    function of 42–43
    gas pedal 43
    high back 42, 43, 55
    screwdriver 37, 42
    step-in 42

strapping into board 56–57
two-strap 42
biomechanics 22, 25, 42, 52, 74
    see also: balance; body
        movements
board
    bidirectional 40
    design 115
    directional 41
    female-specific 40
    flattening, see: flattening the
        board
    flex, see: flex
    freeride 41
    freestyle 40
    longer 41
    selection 40–41, 134
    setting stance to 54–55
    shape 23
    shorter 40
    strapping into 56–57
    technology 22, 38–39
    width 40
    see also: footwork; stance
body movements
    extension 58, 73
    flex 25, 58, 72, 77, 106,
        142–143
    "wait, don't rotate" exercise
        108–109
body protectors 36
boots 34, 40, 47
    fit, importance of good 44
    lacing system 45, 56
bumps 125, 133, 138, 141

C

cabin lifts 92
    cable cars 92, 93
carving 70, 100–103
center of gravity 22, 25, 58, 61,
    90, 112–113
chair lifts 26, 92, 93
climbing 62–63
clothing 26, 34–35, 46–47, 138
    impact protection 36
control points 39, 99, 101, 106,
    110, 118
    feeling 98–99
    opposing 104–105, 110–111
    pointing to 102–103, 104–105
    in powder snow 135, 137
    in reduced visibility 133
    riding fakie 114–115
    and steering 116
    "wait, don't rotate" exercise
        108–109
    working 100–101
corridor, the 118–119

D

dehydration 27
diagonal side-slipping 74–75,
    77, 79
drag lifts 92–93
drops 138, 140–141, 142–143, 151

E

edge tilt
    and balance 112–113
    flattening the board 88, 112,
        133

and flex 23
and speed 126–127, 128–129
and steering 85
see also: heel-edge; toe-edge
exercises
double-pointing 104–105
dry-land 104
hands-on-knees 106–107, 118
opposing pressure 110–111,
118–119
practice 62–63
wait, don't rotate 108–109
extension 58, 73
eyeline 54, 55, 59, 73, 124

F
falling down 60–61
"go low and soft" 60
falling leaf
heel-edge 78–79
toe-edge 80–81
feet
angle 53, 54, 55
and balance 58, 71, 77
control 23, 25, 52, 58
pressure control 98, 100,
102, 116–117
see also: boots; control
points; footwork
field of view 54, 55, 59, 73
flat light 133
flattening the board
after jumps 151
edge change 88, 112, 133
heel turn 87
heel-edge garland 83

in kickers 143
in ollie 141
and speed 126–127
toe-edge garland 84
flex 40, 44
and angle difference 53
body 25, 58, 72, 77, 106,
142–143
and edging 23
in powder snow 135
and steering 25, 111
tip-to-tail 39
torsional 39, 81, 87, 107, 115,
129, 131
when turning 113
flotation 41, 134
footwork
carved turn 101
diagonal side-slipping 75,
77, 79
heel-edge falling leaf 79
heel-edge side-slip 71
heel-edge turn 86–87, 90
heel-edge garland 83
linked turns 90–91
speed control 131
toe-edge falling leaf 81
toe-edge garland 84
toe-edge side-slip 73, 77
toe-edge turn 88
see also: feet
freeriding 18–21
board 41
introduction to 146–147
techniques 150–151
tips 148–149

freestyle
board 40
grabs 144–145
introduction to 138–139
kickers 142–143
ollie 140–141, 142, 144
safety 138
funnel, the 116–117

G
garland
heel-edge 82–83
toe-edge 84–85
gliding 63
gloves 35
goggles 35
grabs 144–145
gradient 124

H
hat 34, 46
head position 59, 65, 76, 84, 86,
114
heel edge
diagonal side-slipping 74–75,
79, 86
edge change 86–87
falling leaf 78–79
garland 82–83
side-slipping 70–71, 74–75,
79, 82
support 55
turn 86–87, 89, 90–91, 99,
103, 127, 128, 130
hip position 52, 54, 58, 85,
104, 109

I

ice 133
impact
    absorption 141, 151
    protection 36
indy grab 145

J

jacket 35, 47
jumping 138, 140–141, 142–143,
    151

K

kickers 142–143
knees
    flex 25, 72, 77, 106, 142–143
    position of 59, 70, 79, 80

L

lifts, riding 92–93
linked turns 90–91

M

McNab Pressure Control
    System 98–99
maintenance kit 36, 37
momentum 135
movement
    preparing for 58–59
    starting 62–63
mute grab 145

O

off-piste 37, 148–149
    see also: freeriding

ollie 140–141, 142, 144

P

pants 35, 47, 56, 57
passing 29
pedaling action
    falling leaf 79, 80–81
    garland 82
    heel turn 87
    and steering 110
    toe turn 89
piste
    grading system 28
    markers 133
    rules 28–29
powder skirt 47
powder snow 136–137
    board 135
    deep 41
    speed in 134–135
pressure transfer
    refining 102–103
    see also: control points; flex;
        McNab Pressure Control
        System; steering
probe 37

R

reflective patches 37
riding fakie 114–115

S

safety
    and dehydration 27
    equipment 148
    freeriding tips 148–149
    freestyle boarding 138

leash 34
piste 28–29
    reduced visibility 133
    and speed 29
    sun protection 27
    and weather 26, 46, 132–133
short-radius turns
    corridor 118–119
    funnel 116–117
shoulder
    position 58, 85, 86, 109
    protection 36
side-slipping
    diagonal 74–77, 79, 86
    heel-edge 70–71, 74–75, 79,
        82
    toe-edge 72–73, 81, 84, 89
    turning 70–71
sidecut 39
skating 63, 65
ski patrol 28
skidding 70, 86, 100, 109, 131,
    134
sliding 65, 71, 73, 75, 76, 79
snow
    powder, see: powder snow
    types of 132, 148, 151
snowboard
    park 138
    theory 22–25
    see also: board
solo riding 148
speed
    awareness 126–127
    control 116–117, 118–119,
        124, 128–131